Climate Change and the Governance of Corporations

Climate change represents the most important environmental challenge of our time. Organisations are responding by implementing governance processes and taking action to reduce their own emissions and the emissions from their supply chains and value chains. Yet very little is known about how these efforts contribute to reducing greenhouse gas emissions (if, indeed, they make any substantive contribution at all) or about how they might be harnessed to deliver more ambitious reductions in emissions.

This book explains when and where particular forms of governance intervention – including internal governance processes and external governance pressures – are likely to impact climate change. From this analysis, it offers practical proposals on the climate policy frameworks that need to be in place to facilitate or accelerate changes in corporate behaviour.

The book is truly global: it focuses on the world's 25 largest retailers (including Walmart, Tesco, Carrefour, Sears and Aldi) and is based on detailed interviews with senior managers from these corporations, and with key global and national NGOs, corporate responsibility experts, politicians and regulators. These interviews provide clear insights into how external governance pressures and actions (public opinion, regulation, incentives) interact with internal governance conditions (management systems and processes, corporate policies, board/CEO leadership) to change and shape corporate actions on climate change and, in turn, the climate change impacts of these corporations.

This book can be used as a core reference for any courses dealing with corporate governance and business strategy, in particular those relating to climate change and to environmental management more generally. It is also of relevance to business practitioners, public policy makers, investors and NGOs interested in ensuring that companies play a constructive role in the transition to a low-carbon economy.

Rory Sullivan is CEO of Chronos Sustainability, Visiting Professor in Practice at the London School of Economics and Political Science (LSE), Senior Associate at the Cambridge Institute for Sustainability Leadership, and General Editor of the Routledge Responsible Investment series. He is an internationally recognised expert on climate change, human rights and investment, with over 30 years' experience in the public and private sectors on these issues.

Andy Gouldson is Professor of Environmental Policy at the University of Leeds and an adjunct professor in the Department for Architecture and Planning at the Norwegian University of Science and Technology (NTNU). His previous roles include Director of the Sustainability Research Institute at the University of Leeds and the ESRC Centre for Climate Change Economics and Policy, and most recently as Dean for Inter-Disciplinary Research at the University of Leeds.

The Responsible Investment Series
Series Editor: Rory Sullivan

The ground-breaking **Responsible Investment** series provides a forum for outstanding empirical and theoretical work on all aspects of responsible investment, allowing the tensions and practical realities of responsible investment to be addressed in a readable, robust and conceptually and empirically rigorous format.

Subject areas covered include:

- The financial, environmental, social and governance outcomes from responsible investment.
- Responsible investment in different asset classes.
- Responsible investment in different geographies.
- The implementation of responsible investment by different actors (e.g. pension funds, asset managers, sovereign wealth funds, private equity funds, insurance companies), and in different geographic regions.
- The role that has been played by collaborative initiatives such as the UN Principles for Responsible Investment, UNEPFI and the investor networks on climate change.
- Public policy and responsible investment.

The Business of Farm Animal Welfare
Edited by Nicky Amos, Rory Sullivan

Principles and Practice of Impact Investing: A Catalytic Revolution
Edited by Veronica Vecchi, Luciano Balbo, Manuela Brusoni, Stefano Caselli

The Responsible Investor Handbook: Mobilizing Workers' Capital for a Sustainable World
By Thomas Croft, Annie Malhotra

The Long Hedge: Preserving Organisational Value through Climate Change Adaptation
By Jason West

Dilemmas in Responsible Investment
By Céline Louche, Steve Lydenberg

Valuing Corporate Responsibility: How Do Investors Really Use Corporate Responsibility Information?
By Rory Sullivan

Responsible Investment
Edited by Rory Sullivan, Craig Mackenzie

Climate Change and the Governance of Corporations: Lessons from the Retail Sector
By Rory Sullivan and Andy Gouldson

Climate Change and the Governance of Corporations

Lessons from the Retail Sector

Rory Sullivan and Andy Gouldson

Routledge
Taylor & Francis Group

LONDON AND NEW YORK

First published 2021
by Routledge
2 Park Square, Milton Park, Abingdon, Oxon OX14 4RN

and by Routledge
52 Vanderbilt Avenue, New York, NY 10017

Routledge is an imprint of the Taylor & Francis Group, an informa business

© 2021 Rory Sullivan and Andy Gouldson

British Library Cataloguing in Publication Data
A catalogue record for this book is available from the British Library

Library of Congress Cataloging-in-Publication Data
Names: Sullivan, Rory, 1968- author. | Gouldson, Andy, 1968- author.
Title: Climate change and corporate governance : lessons from the retail
sector / Rory Sullivan and Andy Gouldson.
Description: Abingdon, Oxon ; New York, NY : Routledge, 2020. | Includes
bibliographical references and index.
Identifiers: LCCN 2020006032 (print) | LCCN 2020006033 (ebook) | ISBN
9780367497187 (hbk) | ISBN 9781003047124 (ebk)
Subjects: LCSH: Retail trade–Environmental aspects. | Climate
change–Environmental aspects. | Corporate governance. | Environmental
responsibility. | Social responsibility of business.
Classification: LCC HF5429 .S8155 2020 (print) | LCC HF5429 (ebook) | DDC
658.4/083–dc23
LC record available at https://lccn.loc.gov/2020006032
LC ebook record available at https://lccn.loc.gov/2020006033

ISBN: 978-0-367-49718-7 (hbk)
ISBN: 978-1-003-04712-4 (ebk)

Typeset in Bembo
by Taylor & Francis Books

To Melinda, Claire and Laura

Rory Sullivan

To Esther, Oscar and Isla

Andy Gouldson

Contents

Illustrations

Acknowledgements

This book is one output from a programme of work funded by the UK Economic and Social Research Council (ESRC) through the Centre for Climate Change Economics and Policy (CCCEP), which is jointly hosted by the University of Leeds and the London School of Economics and Political Science (LSE). In Appendix 2, we describe CCCEP and the Governance Beyond the State project on which this book is based.

We are very grateful to the ESRC for the funding, to the friends and colleagues in CCCEP who helped us to frame and conduct the research and develop the findings, and to all those who contributed to this project through participating in interviews or providing data and information.

We would particularly like to thank: Stavros Afionis, Nicky Amos, Holly Angell, Ralf Barkemeyer, Mike Barry, Martin Cooke, Jack Cunningham, Simon Dietz, Baran Doda, Olga Emelianova, Nathan Fabian, Ulrike Funk, Dexter Galvin, Caterina Gennaoili, Ross Gillard, Richard Gillies, Bob Gordon, David Grover, Margo Hanson, Lisa Häuser, Erin Hiatt, Jemima Jewell, Tracey Jones, Naomi Kissman, Kazutaka Kuroda, Gemma Lacey, Tim Lang, Linda-Eling Lee, Dax Lovegrove, Adam Matthews, Martina Macpherson, Jouni Paavola, Stephanie Pfeifer, Isabelle Reinery, Andrew Sentance, Adam Siegel, Andrew Sudmant, Brendan Sweeney, Laura Timlin, Kené Umeasiegbn, James Van Alstine, Jorien van Hoogen, Helena Viñes Fiestas, Julian Walker-Palin, Lucy Yates and Andrew Yeo.

Finally, as always, we would like to thank our families for their support, love and patience.

Acronyms

AFGC	Australian Food and Grocery Council
ANRA	Australian National Retailers' Association
ARA	Australian Retailers Association
CDP	(previously) Carbon Disclosure Project
CCCEP	Centre for Climate Change Economics and Policy
CO_2	carbon dioxide
DECC	(UK) Department of Energy and Climate Change
ESAA	Electricity Supply Association of Australia
ESRC	Economic and Social Research Council
EU	European Union
IEEP	Institute for European Environmental Policy
IPCC	Intergovernmental Panel on Climate Change
JCSA	Japan Chain Stores Association
JFCA	Japan Franchise Chain Association
LSE	London School of Economics and Political Science
NGO	non-governmental organisation
NRDC	Natural Resources Defense Council
RCP	Representative Concentration Pathway
RILA	Retail Industry Leaders Association
SDC	Sustainable Development Commission
UK	United Kingdom
UN	United Nations
UNDP	UN Development Programme
UNEP	UN Environment Programme
UNEP FI	UNEP Finance Initiative
US	United States of America
USDA	US Department of Agriculture
USEPA	US Environmental Protection Agency
WMO	World Meteorological Organisation

About the authors

Dr Rory Sullivan is CEO of Chronos Sustainability – a specialist advisory firm which delivers transformative, systemic change in the social and environmental performance of key industry sectors – and Visiting Professor in Practice at the Grantham Research Institute on Climate Change and the Environment at the London School of Economics and Political Science (LSE). He is an internationally recognised expert on climate finance and responsible investment. He has worked extensively with a range of organisations – including UNEP FI, the World Economic Forum, UNDP, the Principles for Responsible Investment, the Transition Pathway Initiative, the Institutional Investors Group on Climate Change, the World Bank and the OECD – as well as with national governments and many private sector and civil society organisations on issues such as corporate sustainability, climate change and responsible investment. He is the author/editor of eight books, over 40 peer-reviewed journal articles, over 50 book chapters and many reports and articles on climate change and investment issues.

Andy Gouldson is Professor of Environmental Policy at the University of Leeds. He is an inter-disciplinary environmental social scientist whose work combines aspects of geography and environment, politics and policy, economics and management and science and technology studies. His main area of expertise relates to the influence of different forms of policy and governance on businesses, on economic development and on the relationships between environment, economy and society. He has also worked extensively on the management of environmental risks and on theories of ecological modernisation and environmental justice. Much of his work has focused on issues relating to air pollution, and more recently he has focused on the management of the risks associated with climate change and on enhancing the prospects for a transition towards a low-carbon economy. He was one of the founding directors of the ESRC Centre for Climate Change Economics and Policy and of the ESRC Place-based Climate Action Network. He has been Editor of the journal *Environmental Policy and Governance* (formerly *European Environment*) since 1991.

1 Introduction

Climate change represents the most important environmental challenge of our time. There is societal, political, investor and corporate understanding that the climate crisis is accelerating, with profound implications for our lives, and the lives of our children and grandchildren.

The role and contribution of business is now central to debates about how we as society act on climate change. Companies emit large quantities of greenhouse gases from their own activities and operations. The goods, products and services that they produce and the behaviours that they encourage or enable have direct implications – which may be positive or negative – for global greenhouse gas emissions. Companies themselves are also affected by climate change. Efforts to reduce greenhouse gas emissions may create opportunities, such as for renewable energy or for new energy-saving technologies. These efforts may result in particular products or services no longer being viable, as a consequence for example of changes in regulation (e.g. taxes and charges on petrol and diesel-fuelled vehicles), in the economics of alternative products (e.g. in many locations, solar and wind power generation technologies are now cost competitive with traditional fossil fuels) or changes in consumer demand (e.g. the rise of vegetarianism and veganism). The physical impacts of climate change bring further challenges; companies may need to invest to ensure that their assets are protected from flood risk and extreme weather conditions, they may need to diversify their supply chains to avoid disruption, and they may benefit from investments made by governments and other companies in flood protection.

In parallel to the growth in understanding of the importance of companies to climate change and the importance of climate change to companies, we have seen a growth in enthusiasm among policymakers and other stakeholders to harness the power and influence of corporations to deliver or support the delivery of societal goals on climate change, as set out in the Paris Agreement on Climate Change. We have seen an upsurge in policy interventions including traditional regulatory interventions such as energy efficiency standards, market-based instruments such as emissions trading schemes and environmental taxes, disclosure requirements such as corporate greenhouse emissions reporting and integrated reporting, and voluntary initiatives such as science-based targets and collaborative investor engagement programmes. Some of these have been focused directly at companies; others have been indirect, focused on changing the incentives provided to companies or enabling other actors to press companies to take action. Some have been mandatory, and others have been voluntary. Some have involved government, whereas others have been led by others (e.g. NGO campaigns, investor engagement, voluntary corporate initiatives).

Some elements of this changing context for the governance of corporations are comparatively well understood. Research on political science and public policy tells us a lot about the influence of different forms or policy or regulation on business behaviour. Research on management and business studies offers important insights into the influence of the structures, systems and cultures that exist within corporations. However, we know much less about the actual or potential influence that other forms of governance can have on corporate behaviour. We know even less about the ways in which all of these different forms of governance interact or conspire to shape the broader climate for the governance of corporations, about the effectiveness of different forms of governance or about the extent to which we can rely on them to deliver social objectives.

Despite how little is known about how these governance mechanisms work (or indeed whether they work at all), we appear to be seeing an acceleration in the rate at which they are being deployed by governments. This acceleration is driven, at least in part, by the desire of many governments to avoid introducing regulation, instead looking to other actors or to companies themselves to fill the regulatory role that has traditionally been played by government. It is also driven by some of the perceived advantages of these new forms of governance: more efficient, lower transaction costs, empowering consumers and other actors, flexibility, speed of implementation.

The consequence is that, in many contexts, we are embarking on wholesale experiments with new forms of governance without really knowing whether, to what extent or under what conditions, they might actually work. Similarly, relatively little is known about the role that corporate action could play in the fight against climate change. There are multiple case-studies of the actions taken by individual companies but limited analysis of the role that could be played by the corporate sector as a whole, or by distinct sectors within the wider economy in the fight against climate change. There is a vague sense that 'something must be done' but no clear sense about how companies might be engaged with or of the outcomes that might be delivered through this engagement. Put another way, we are searching for companies to play their role in helping solve the climate crisis, with only the vaguest of understandings of what role they might play, what the limits to their role might be, how we might enable them to play this role, or who need to be involved.

The central question considered in this book is whether, to what extent and under what conditions new forms of governance can ensure that corporations make a fuller contribution to the realisation of public interest objectives, with a particular focus on public interest objectives relating to climate change.

In this book, we focus on a particular sector (the supermarket/retail sector) and the evolution of its response to climate change over a 15-year period, from 2000 through to 2015. This was a period characterised by significant change in the regulatory/policy context within which this sector operated, by significant experimentation and innovation within these firms, and by a dramatic change in the corporate narrative around climate change.

Why retail?

Why is the retail sector important and why is it relevant? There are a number of reasons. Retailers touch the lives of billions of people every day, through the goods that they purchase and provide and through the relationships they have with their suppliers, employees and customers. Retail is one of the most economically significant sectors in virtually every country in the world. Retailers, individually and collectively, have a huge carbon footprint; this comprises both their own direct footprint through their buildings, their logistics and their other infrastructure and the wider footprint associated with the goods that they provide and the manner in which these goods are used, consumed and disposed of by their customers. How big is this footprint? In the UK it is estimated that the sector's own footprint accounts for approximately 1% of the UK's greenhouse gas emissions but that emissions from its value and supply chains could be ten times larger.

The sector is of interest because, despite being comparatively unregulated through traditional forms of government policy, the sector as a whole and individual companies within the sector have made commitments to and delivered substantial improvements in their environmental/carbon performance. The obvious factors that have led to them making these commitments and delivering these changes have included competitive pressures and the need to achieve competitive advantage, the indirect consequences of regulation in other sectors of the economy (e.g. energy sector regulation), consumer pressure and NGO campaigns. But there have also been other factors at play, many of which sit relatively unseen within these corporations; these include the personal motivations and interests of senior leaders within the organisation, internal governance processes that enable or hinder change, and the consequences of building knowledge and expertise within the organisation.

Finally, many companies have characteristics that are similar to those in the retail sector; they have long and complex supply chains, they have extensive interactions with and influence on their customers, and they face relatively little regulatory attention on their environmental or climate change performance. Retailers are both the source and the objects of numerous other non-state governance pressures; they govern themselves, their supply chains and the choices and impacts of their customers, but they are also governed by market conditions, societal expectations, media representations, customer concerns, various private standards and voluntary codes and so on. As such, many of the wider conclusions about how governance processes function within the retail sector are likely to be highly relevant to many other sectors and companies.

An overview of the structure and content of this book

We have divided this book into three main parts. In the first part – Chapters 2 and 3 – we provide a framework for analysing how governance processes might influence corporate practice and performance. Chapter 2 discusses and describes the relationship between the state and the corporation. It discusses the influence and the strength of the influence that the state might exert, and discusses how this has changed and might be changing. It also reflects on the corporation's view on social responsibility and the corporation's own internal (or corporate) governance processes, defines how the corporation might respond to the influence exerted by the state and, in turn, considers the impact the corporation has on society. Chapter 3 extends this analysis to consider the potential influence of other actors (e.g. NGOs), and presents a model of the interaction between external governance processes (or pressures) and internal governance systems. This analysis of the interactions is used to explain how corporations are likely to respond, the actions they will take and the impacts that they will have.

In the second part we present two empirical case-studies, both of which focus on the retail sector. In Chapter 4 we discuss and analyse how the major UK retailers have responded to climate change in the period 2000 to 2015. We analyse the policy and other drivers for action, the internal factors that have affected the corporations' responses, the actions they have taken and the impacts these actions have had on each company's current and future greenhouse gas emissions. In Chapter 5, we present a similar analysis for the world's largest retailers. We break this chapter down by geography, considering each of the United States, France, Germany, Japan and Australia. The full list of companies we cover is presented in Table 1.1, and we discuss our research process and analysis in Appendix 1.

In the third part, we discuss the implications of our analysis. Chapter 6 discusses the implications for the governance of corporations, asking what lessons we can draw about the design and implementation of policy, campaigns and other programmes directed at driving change within corporations, and about

Table 1.1 List of companies covered

Aeon (Japan)	J Sainsbury (UK)	Schwarz/Lidl (Germany)
ALDI (Germany)	Koninklijke Ahold	Sears (US)
Best Buy (US)	(Netherlands)	Seven & I (Japan)
Carrefour (France)	Kroger (US)	Target (US)
Co-operative Group (UK)	Lowe's (US)	Tesco (UK)
Costco (US)	Marks and Spencer (UK)	Waitrose (UK)
CVS Caremark (US)	Metro (Germany)	Walgreen Company (US)
E Leclerc (France)	Morrisons (UK)	Walmart/Asda (US)
Edeka (Germany)	REWE Group (Germany)	Wesfarmers (Australia)
Groupe Auchan (France)	Safeway (US)	Woolworths (Australia)
Home Depot (US)		

the design and implementation of internal governance processes. Chapter 7 reflects on the specific case of climate change and what the theoretical analysis and empirical evidence tell us about the potential contribution that companies can make to action on climate change, and how governments and other stakeholders can maximise the contribution that is made by companies. In this chapter, we also reflect on how governance mechanisms and processes need to evolve over time, to enable us to respond effectively to climate change while avoiding the risk of being locked in to current business models and practices.

2 Understanding the governance relationship between the state and corporations

What do we mean by governance?

At its simplest, governance refers to the ability of any public, private or civic actor to regulate or influence either its own behaviour or performance or those of another. When we look at corporations, this definition recognises that corporations can be governed by multiple forms of government policy, by the actions of private actors such as investors, insurers and trading partners and by those of civic actors such as pressure groups, the media or local communities. The definition also recognises the importance of self-regulation and the influence that the corporate governance structures, systems and cultures can have on business behaviour.

Of course, all of these governing influences have long existed. But in many contexts the governance roles played by actors around and within corporations are evolving. This is especially evident where governments are unwilling or unable to regulate in traditional ways and where private or civic actors are trying to step in to exert influence in different ways.

Why do we need to govern corporations?

Clearly, there are some areas where private and public interests coincide so that the pursuit of corporate self-interest can lead to outcomes that are socially desirable. Corporations can, and frequently do, provide important goods and services, create employment, pay wages and taxes, pursue innovation, provide infrastructures and so on. Many companies have looked to move beyond the benefits that flow from their core business activities to deliver additional socially desirable outcomes; they often use terms such as corporate social responsibility and 'shared value' to describe these efforts.

Despite these important contributions, there are significant areas where private and public interests do not coincide and where the exercise of corporate self-interest can result in outcomes that are at odds with broader social objectives. Corporations can play an important role in creating or exacerbating social, economic and environmental problems. They have been criticised because their core business activities fail to deliver benefits on the scale that might be expected; they have found themselves questioned because of the quantity and quality of the jobs that they create, the level of wages and taxes they pay, the impacts of the technologies they create, the value and accessibility of the infrastructures they provide, and so on. Beyond the debates about the specific activities of individual companies are deeper concerns about the structural impacts of the broader social, economic and political systems that they have helped to create and sustain; for example, companies have an influence on patterns of consumption, on policy and regulation, on local and regional economic development, and on the shape and structure of society.

Overall, therefore, corporations play a central but highly ambiguous role in modern society. It is also clear that different forms of governance play an important role in shaping their impact. However, perspectives on governance differ; four particular clusters of thought – which we discuss further below – can be discerned in the debate on the governance of corporations:

- The Reconfigured State: Some argue that although the specific governance roles played by different actors in the public, private and civic sectors are changing, the overall level of influence that society can exert need not change.
- The Retreat of the State: Others with a more critical view argue that we are witnessing a retreat of the state and a dismantling of regulatory frameworks without being sure that any effective alternatives are in place.
- Reinvigoration Beyond the State: Those with a more hopeful stance see the potential for new forms of governance to emerge that can help to ensure that social demands are more effectively articulated so that private actions make a fuller contribution to public interests.
- Governance from the Inside: Those with more interest in what happens in and around corporations stress the potential that the structures and systems associated with corporate governance can play in delivering corporate social responsibility.

Perspective 1: the reconfigured state

In most jurisdictions, the state has long played a central role in governing private and public interests and in balancing individual freedoms with collective responsibilities. Depending on the jurisdiction, different levels and forms of government policy have been relied upon to accentuate the positive and mitigate the negative impacts of corporate behaviour. The role of the state in mediating what are sometimes coinciding and sometimes competing interests clearly varies significantly across time and space.

It is, however, now widely argued that many states are moving away from a controlling role and that in some but not all instances they are adopting an enabling role. This shift means that these governments are less likely to regulate private interests or defend the public interest. Instead, they are more likely to seek to both encourage new forms of self-regulation and to enable non-state actors to act as quasi-regulators. The latter may include companies seeking to influence their suppliers, their customers and other entities with whom they have commercial relationships.

In such situations, the governance of private actors and of private actions relies much less on government and much more on self-regulation and on new forms of private or civic regulation. Self-regulation happens when an actor chooses to govern its own behaviour or performance. Private regulation comes, for example, through the influence that various private actors can have on the companies they invest in, insure, purchase from, trade with, provide services to or report on. Civic regulation comes from NGO, media, community or consumer pressure or from the ability of society at large to grant or withhold some kind of social licence to operate from private actors.

Sometimes self-regulation and private or civic regulation ('governance beyond the state') can emerge and function effectively in the absence of any encouragement or support from the state. More often, however, these forms of regulation depend on the state playing an enabling or facilitating role through, for example, defining and enforcing property rights, providing economic and other incentives, and requiring disclosures that enable other actors to hold corporations to account.

Of course, governance mechanisms do not emerge or exist in isolation. In practice, different forms of public, private, civic and self-governance co-exist and interact in dynamic and complex ways. This means that specific actors or forms of behaviour are likely to be shaped by cocktails of different governing influences – or, in other words, by hybrid governance arrangements that combine aspects of public, private, civic and self-regulation.

The emergence of these new governance arrangements can be seen as changing the predominant form of regulation applied to mediate private and public relations and as changing the actors who are expected to do the governing or regulating. However, these changes, at least in theory, do not necessarily affect the overall level of control or influence being exerted. In principle, new forms of governance could deliver similar outcomes to more traditional approaches (such as regulation). In seeking to use their limited resources wisely, states can – again, at least in theory – switch from being the routine regulator of first resort to being the responsive regulator of last resort. A responsive state's first preference is for self-regulation; its second is for forms of private and civic regulation that do not depend on the state; its third is for forms of private and civic regulation that can be enabled by but that operate beyond the state; and its fourth and final preference, to be adopted when all other options have been shown to be ineffective, is for traditional state-based regulation.

In other words, states with limited appetites or capacities for regulation might hope that the emergence of new governance possibilities and of new governance actors (or new quasi-regulators) might allow them to leave much of the regulating of private actors to other parties and to only step in to protect the public interest when absolutely necessary. This relies on the assumption that private actors are sometimes willing and able to govern their own behaviour and/or that non-state private or civic actors are willing and able to step in to do some regulating or governing, possibly with some support from an enabling government. If the overall level of control or influence is to be maintained, there must be either the potential for these new forms of self, private or civic regulation to be as effective as older forms of state-centred regulation, or the potential for states to be able to monitor the effectiveness of new governance arrangements and to be able to step in quickly where they are not working.

Perspective 2: the retreat of the state

Many of these assumptions – i.e. that private actors are willing and able to govern their own behaviour, that non-state private or civic actors are willing and able to act as quasi-regulators, that states can intervene quickly and effectively if needed – can readily be questioned. In fact, the emergence of new forms of governance could be interpreted as a retreat of the state (Strange, 1996) and as an abdication by the state of the role that it should be playing in protecting the public interest. In such a view, it is highly optimistic that private actors will readily self-regulate to a consistently high standard, that other private or civic actors will be willing or able to mobilise and become quasi-regulators (even with support from an enabling state) or that government will be able to act responsively and to step in where needed. Of particular importance here is the risk that, by encouraging self-regulation and divesting itself of specific regulatory powers, the state may lose its ability to monitor the impacts of a large number of non-state governance arrangements or to revert back to a state-based approach where necessary. Indeed, the emergence of new forms of governance, or even simply the withdrawal of the state from certain aspects of regulation and enforcement, could enable or accelerate a further retreat of the state (Lewis, 2018).

These challenges raise questions about the extent to which we can rely on these new governance arrangements to deliver public interest objectives. They highlight the potential for highly variable outcomes that will affect different social groups in different ways. It can be argued that those actors and groups that are able to mobilise to ensure their interests are protected will do so, but that those who cannot will be left more exposed by a weakened and fragmented governance system that allows private actors to pursue their goals more freely, even at the expense of the public interest. This leads to significant concerns about the reliability and transparency of the new governance arrangements, and the motivation and accountability of the multitude of non-state actors that are involved in them.

The conclusion that follows from this more critical perspective is that many states are abandoning an older state-centred approach to engage in a risky experiment with new governance arrangements. The older state-centred approach had a democratic basis and a level of legitimacy and accountability. It used established institutions and instruments in a broad-based attempt to protect the public interest. New governance arrangements, by contrast, tend to cede and disperse powers to a multitude of different actors with a wide range of motivations, who can act in uncoordinated ways, who can lack legitimacy and accountability and who may or may not have the capacity or commitment to try and ensure that corporations make a fuller contribution to society.

These new governance arrangements can, therefore, be portrayed as being at best highly uncertain and at worst doomed to failure. Those who see this outcome as being in the interests of the corporations who were previously the targets of state-centred regulation see signs of a captured or captive state here (Hertel-Fernandez, 2019; Monbiot, 2000) where, rather than regulating private interests for public ends, the state has been persuaded that the best way to further the public interest is to free up private actors to pursue their interests more freely. This leads to a form of state failure where alliances between powerful private interests and government systematically limit the extent to which government is willing to intervene on behalf of the public interest.

A further criticism that could be levelled at these new governance arrangements is the likelihood of regulatory capture. This is a common criticism of state-based regulation, where state-based regulators may be susceptible to being captured by the interests of the actors they were supposed to be regulating. A sceptical analysis of the potential of new governance arrangements might conclude that there is an even more significant opportunity for what we might term 'governance capture', where the new non-state actors that we hope will play a role in protecting the public interest become overly sympathetic to the interests and concerns of the private actors they are somehow seeking to influence, leaving only an illusion of control.

Perspective 3: reinvigoration beyond the state

The proponents of new forms of governance see many instances where governments fail by being reluctant, unwilling or slow to act or where their actions are ineffective, inefficient or inequitable or have unintended side-effects (Gouldson and Murphy, 1998). They argue that new forms of governance can fill the gaps left through the retreat or failures of the state. They stress both the need and the opportunity to move away from a reliance on older forms of government intervention – especially those that come from monolithic nation states – and instead emphasise the potential for what have been termed 'polycentric governance arrangements' (Jordan et al., 2015; Ostrom, 2005, 2010).

These forms of governance are multi-level and multi-actor in their composition. They suggest that capacities to control, coordinate or steer different forms of social and economic life are no longer concentrated in the nation state, but are instead diffused upwards to the global scale, downwards to the local level and outwards to non-state actors (Bache and Flinders, 2005; Black, 2008; Kooiman, 2003; Wurzel et al., 2013). Consequently, it is argued that social and economic activities are increasingly being governed through what have been termed polycentric networks that operate across multiple scales and in diverse arenas and that combine different forms of public, private and civic action (Paavola et al., 2009; Ostrom, 2010). The argument is that, by strengthening linkages between international, national, regional or local scales, new governance arrangements can enable the much more effective implementation or delivery of higher-level initiatives. Furthermore, at least in principle, a wider range of actors may be engaged in the governance process if there is a move away from a top-down hierarchical view and, instead, subsidiarity and some bottom-up dimensions are designed into the process. This may, in turn, result in more effective, legitimate and equitable processes and outcomes, allow more responsive, adaptable and rapid responses to pressing problems, and result in tailored responses that reflect the diversity of issues and conditions in different contexts. Such flexibility may also encourage experimentation with alternative approaches, which can play an important role in learning or problem solving and in transferring good practice.

A further benefit of polycentric governance arrangements is that they offer the potential to be based not on hierarchies and the articulation of power but on networks and collaboration or cooperation. Governance networks can enlist new participants and enable communication, build commitment and strengthen capacities for both individual and collective action. These new forms of governance can help build trust or social capital in different networks or communities (Ostrom, 2010). Trust and social capital can accumulate over time and be associated with the emergence of self-reinforcing institutions that can be effective in establishing new social values and norms. Where these values and norms are embedded in organisations such as corporations, they can trigger more effective self-regulatory approaches. These may also be more durable as they are driven from within rather than being dependent on external pressures.

The proliferation of new forms of governance in different contexts and multiple domains could then lead to multiple overlapping governance frameworks. In principle, different frameworks with different goals could at least co-exist; they are likely to interact and, in some instances, they could even fuse and become self-reinforcing (Jordan et al., 2015). If so, then to some extent the argument that new forms of governance may deliver improved outcomes aligns with the argument that we are seeing a reconfiguration of the roles played by different actors but not necessarily a reduction in the aggregated level of influence that can be exerted. If those new governance arrangements are at least as effective, efficient and equitable as the state-centred approaches that preceded them, then the public interest could be more effectively furthered through the adoption of new governance arrangements.

The emergence of new forms of governance could also mean that different frameworks duplicate or compete with each other, and some frameworks could displace or undermine others. It seems likely that the emergence of new governance frameworks will have dynamic impacts and that these will determine whether new forms of governance will be a supplement to or a substitute for state action. A key issue though is that forms of governance beyond or without the state could create a form of moral hazard for governments as they offer an excuse for the state not to act, thereby reinforcing a philosophy that emphasises the role of small states, free markets and the big society. However, at this point, this is a speculative conclusion as the interactions between different governance frameworks are barely understood and there is limited knowledge or evidence on the different ways in which they might interact, let alone on what the diverse effects of these interactions might be.

Perspective 4: governance from the inside

Much of the literature on public, private or civic governance focuses on what happens outside the corporation, and pays limited attention to what happens inside the corporation. This is a clear omission as the conditions within the corporation will have a critical influence on whether and how governance interventions work and on the outcomes, if any, that result from these interventions.

There is a significant literature on the governance processes within corporations (or 'corporate governance'), although it often pays limited attention to the external governance pressures and influences acting on the corporation. In its broadest sense, corporate governance refers to the systems through which corporate activities are directed and controlled (Cadbury Committee, 1992). Traditional conceptions of corporate governance – at least for larger publicly owned or listed firms – place particular emphasis on the ownership, management and accountability structures of companies. They emphasise the importance of the systems that are put in place in all larger companies to manage, monitor, audit and ensure the integrity of their performance and to generate the data needed to enable their shareholders and regulators – and, increasingly, other stakeholders – to hold the company and its managers to account (Monks and Minnow, 2011).

Corporate governance structures should therefore enable companies to manage their behaviour and performance, to demonstrate compliance with relevant laws and to deliver any other obligations that they need to meet. For many, laws and regulations are seen as the formal articulation of society's concerns and expectations and, as such, set the boundaries for corporate activity. In fact, it is frequently argued that as long as a company complies with relevant laws, it should be free to pursue its private interests and to maximise returns on investment for shareholders. However, this narrow view is increasingly challenged, with some business leaders arguing that corporations need to pay much more explicit attention to the needs and interests of their stakeholders, not just their shareholders (see, for example, Business Roundtable, 2019).

Debates on governance complicate this stance somewhat as the consequences of a widespread replacement of hard law with softer forms of governance have yet to be fully understood. One attempt to frame these discussions is through the quasi-legalism of notions of a 'social licence' or a 'licence to operate' (see, for example, Morrison, 2014). These notions suggest that society somehow has the capacity to set and implement standards and then to monitor performance and sanction non-compliance. In that context, corporate governance systems could be asked to deliver compliance not only with hard law but also with the expectations of new forms of governance such as those defined in private standards and codes of conduct. This is not a theoretical argument; companies, through their commitments to concepts such as corporate responsibility and shared value, have to some extent at least accepted that they need to make some contribution to the public interest, for example in areas relating to social responsibility or sustainability.

One of the key limits (or boundaries) to efforts to impose any sort of social responsibilities on companies relates to the need for there to be a business case for action. One of the central tenets of corporate governance in most market-based economies is that company directors have a duty to maximise shareholder value, with this duty generally defined in relatively narrow financial terms. The framing of duties in this way, at its narrowest, is often interpreted as meaning that, after compliance with relevant laws, the only outcome that matters is direct, short-term returns on investment. Any calls for corporations to make wider contributions to the public interest but that do not also make a direct contribution to shareholder value may therefore clash with these duties to maximise shareholder value and thus be inadmissible. Indeed, in highly com-petitive or cost-sensitive markets, doing anything other than maximising shareholder value might even threaten the viability of the business.

Fortunately, the picture is not quite as stark as this argument would suggest. Even in a narrow financial frame of reference, it can often be argued that longer-term shareholder returns can depend upon strategic engagement with stakeholder or broader social concerns (Chesebrough and Sullivan, 2017; Sullivan et al., 2019). A business cannot survive in the longer term if it is out of step with the values of the society within which it operates. This argument points to the need for companies to take a more strategic and longer-term approach to their engagement with stakeholders and with the wider public interest.

Corporations are not monolithic and different businesses respond to similar agendas and governance pressures in different ways. Corporate cultures play a vital role in shaping corporate behaviour. These corporate cultures can be shaped by the broader social context and by the values set out by the owners, managers, employees and customers of the firm. A company's stakeholders can therefore mobilise to make social concerns significant to the corporation in a wide range of ways, for example by deciding who they invest in, work for or buy from. Where they do this, they can reshape the boundaries of feasible action – or the limits of what can be done within the limits of the business case for action – and, thereby, change the context for corporate decision making.

This offers another route through which corporations can be governed, and one that can be enabled by government, particularly through laws on access to information or rights to participate in corporate decision making. For share-holders with an interest in the financial performance of firms, governments have long recognised that stock markets depend on access to reliable, consistent forms of information. Underpinned by legislation, whole industries of accounting and audit have emerged to meet these needs. In some instances, similar approaches are being extended to stakeholders with an interest in the social or environmental performance of firms. Certainly, if broader forms of governance are to be effective in ensuring that the private activities of corporations contribute to public interests, then the right to information needs to be expanded. This is another illustration of the central role that an enabling state can play in creating the conditions within which new forms of governance can work.

Therefore, one way of thinking about corporate governance is to see corporate structures and systems, and cultures and values, as mechanisms that enable corporations to comply with relevant laws and to contribute to broader social objectives. Although the extent to which they might contribute to the public interest can be constrained by the duties imposed on their directors and by the limits of the business case, there are multiple ways in which companies' behaviour and performance can be influenced by the societies within which they operate. Within this, government can play a key role in creating the context for corporate governance and in enabling new forms of shareholder influence or corporate accountability.

Concluding comments

So, which of these four perspectives is true? Are we seeing a change in the nature but not in the level of regulation or governance of corporations or are we seeing a dismantling of the regulatory functions of the state with no effective alternative in place? Is there a proliferation of new forms of governance that enable non-state actors to reach the areas that states will not or cannot reach? Can we rely on the structures and systems of corporate governance to ensure that they contribute to the public interest?

Much of the literature on this question has focused on whether or not this transition from state-based to other forms of regulation is happening and, if so, what its key features might be. Much less emphasis has been placed on assessing whether, or to what extent or under what conditions, these new governance arrangements might actually work; we actually know surprisingly little about the ways in which different forms of governance interact and exert influence over specific actors (Gouldson and Sullivan, 2014). That is, how effective might they be in ensuring that the private lives of corporations create outcomes that are in the public interest?

3 Understanding the relationship and interactions between internal and external governance processes

In Chapter 2, we discussed some of the features of the new governance landscape. We concluded that we actually know quite little about how different forms of governance interact and influence corporations. In this chapter, we look more closely at the forms of governance that exist both around and within corporations. We propose a simple conceptual framework or heuristic that helps us to consider the ways in which, and the extent to which, these external and internal governance forms conspire to shape corporate behaviour. For simplicity we start with what we describe as governance from the outside, where public, private and civic actors engage in activities that seek to shape the behaviour or performance of a corporation. We then focus on governance from the inside, where we discuss those factors – these will include structures, systems, policies, processes, resources, opportunities, cultures, values – that shape the behaviour of the corporation and its response to external pressures. We conclude by presenting a simple framework that allows us both to describe the internal and external governance pressures acting on a corporation and to explain how these internal and external processes interact.

Governance from the outside

As we discussed in Chapter 2, the debates on governance in political science and related fields have tended to focus on questions about the changing role of national governments. The question of whether the regulatory powers of nation states are in retreat or decline – for example in the face of globalisation and neo-liberalisation, or recession and austerity – has been the focus of much debate. Some have argued that rather than shrinking in the face of such challenges, governments have innovated, for example through the introduction of new policy instruments that seek to mobilise and harness the governing powers of markets and civil society (Wurzel et al., 2013), or through initiatives that 'decentre' the state by rescaling its powers across different levels and by distributing them among different actors (Black, 2008; Jessop, 2004). However, there are certainly instances where the powers of nation states are being diminished, and in such instances it is frequently argued that there is increased dependence on non-state actors to help to take decisions, regulate behaviours or deliver initiatives that are in the public interest (see, for example, Falkner, 2003; Gouldson and Bebbington, 2007). Whether private and civic actors have the inclination or the capacity to assume such roles has been hotly debated, and while many question the potential for civic actors to take up the governing roles that have been left unoccupied by government, at least in some cases we can see the emergence of stronger and more vibrant private and civil society organisations and their active engagement in new forms of governance (Falkner, 2003).

Of course, in many settings we have not seen a complete or even, arguably, that substantial a dismantling of the state. Many traditional forms of state-centred governance still prevail. But it has long been argued that governments (particularly those of a neo-liberal persuasion) are reluctant to draw on their capacities for control, and that they sometimes apply them only as a last resort when other forms of non-state governance have been shown to be unavailable or ineffective (see Ayres and Braithwaite, 1992; Gouldson and Bebbington, 2007). Rather than deploying their own scarce resources, such governments first hope to see social actors engaging in new modes of civic governance, or industry and other market-based actors deploying new forms of private governance. In order to facilitate the efforts of these actors, governments may need to play a facilitating or enabling role through, for example, the provision of incentives or requiring particular disclosures from corporations.

It is relevant to note that many of the new private or civic governance measures that exist beyond the boundaries of the state have not actually relied on the state to either explicitly encourage or explicitly enable their existence (although they often build on pre-existing legal frameworks). Examples could include trade associations that regulate their members, private standards and voluntary codes that offer different forms of certification, and non-governmental organisations (NGOs) and consumer groups that develop new standards and league tables (Busch, 2013; Falkner, 2003; Levy and Newell, 2005; Pattberg, 2007). They include more direct forms of business-to-business regulation, for example where investors seek to influence the performance of the companies they invest in or where large retailers seek to manage the behaviour of their suppliers, and civic arrangements where local communities negotiate controls directly with businesses (Amos and Sullivan, 2018; Gouldson, 2004; Pfeifer and Sullivan, 2008). And they include new forms of stakeholder influence, for example where different groups contest the extent to which some actors have a 'social licence' or a 'licence to operate', or where they seek to create and amplify reputational risks for actors that do not comply with social expectations (Freeman et al., 2010; Morrison, 2014).

These changes create considerable challenges, both practically and for our understanding of the processes and influence of 'new' forms of governance. Under 'old' governance conditions, power was concentrated in the state and so the articulation of power, for example through the application of rules and sanctions, could be relatively straightforward. But under 'new' governance conditions, power is diffused in wider networks, with multiple actors with varying capacities, diverse and often divergent interests and competing logics all seeking to exert influence in different ways (Knox-Hayes and Levy, 2011). Where in the past theory has focused on the potential for coalitions of actors with well-aligned goals to collaborate to secure influence over government policy making (Sabatier and Jenkins-Smith, 1999), we now have to understand the ability of multiple actors in what can be fluid and uncoordinated networks to influence business behaviour. But we also know that businesses are unlikely to be the passive targets of governance interventions – they can deploy a range of tactics to shape the governance conditions under which they operate. In this new world of polycentric governance, the opportunity structures for all actors, and the strategies that they deploy to create and exploit them, have certainly become more diverse and complex.

Governance from the inside

While much has been written about these various forms of 'governance from the outside', surprisingly few links are made between these debates and the mainstream debate on corporate governance. This may be because wider debates on governance tend to be led by political scientists and related disciplines, whereas debates on corporate governance tend to be in the domain of business and management studies. Whatever the reason, this presents a divide or at least a disjuncture in the debate on governance.

As we discussed in Chapter 2, corporate governance refers to the systems through which corporate activities are directed and controlled. More specifically, it refers to the relationships between especially the shareholders and managers of a firm, and possibly also wider stakeholders, and the structures and systems used to take and implement decisions, monitor performance and ensure accountability (Monks and Minnow, 2011). Corporate governance can therefore be interpreted narrowly as referring to the essentially private relationship between the owners and managers of a firm or it can be interpreted more broadly as the relationships between a firm and its wider range of stakeholders, including those in the public, private and civic sectors. In either instance, there is some blurring of the boundary between broader forms of governance and narrower forms of corporate governance, and – because of the role that government regulations play in shaping the context or establishing the legal basis for corporate governance – between private, hybrid and traditionally state-based forms of governance.

Traditional conceptions of corporate governance therefore place particular emphasis on the ownership and management structures of companies, and on the systems that are in place to manage and monitor performance and to generate the data needed to enable shareholders, and possibly stakeholders, to hold the company and its managers to account. From a shareholder perspective, corporate governance is very much about the control of principal-agent problems and the control of corporate behaviour to ensure the maximisation of shareholder value from corporate activities.

In practice, however, it is clear that corporate behaviour and performance are not only governed by such structures and systems. Corporate activities are also shaped by the resources of the firm and the ways that they shape a company's competitive position and the ways in which it interacts with its stakeholders. Resource-based views of the firm suggest that such resources can be tangible (e.g. patents) and intangible (e.g. tacit knowledge), and that they can be transferable (e.g. by developing or buying in new expertise) or contextually specific (e.g. they are not easily imitated, replicated or transplanted) (Barney, 2001; Wernerfelt, 1984, 1995). Different firms generate and draw on different resource endowments in different ways as they seek to create and exploit new opportunities; the consequence is that at least some of the conditions for corporate governance are highly specific and context dependent.

While the resource-based view of the firm tends to emphasise the economic or technological resources of a firm, it is clear that some key political resources also have great value. The ability to shape the governance conditions experienced by the firm is one such political resource. Firms can create shareholder value for themselves by fostering brand loyalty and by building levels of trust and acceptance that protect the firm from reputational risks (Fombrun et al., 2000; Gouldson et al., 2007). They can also exert influence in ways that pre-empt, undermine, capture or curtail the influence of groups that seek to adopt initiatives or impose agendas that threaten the interests of the firm (see for instance Wrigley et al., 2002). And they can seek to ensure that their own logics are embedded in the standards bodies and governance mechanisms that they seek to comply with (Knox-Hayes and Levy, 2011).

More broadly, corporate activities are also governed by the cultures and values that predominate within the organisation as a whole or that exist within particular parts of the organisation or in the individuals that work for it (Kotter and Heskett, 1992; Ravasi and Schultz, 2006). These cultures and values can guide the ways in which the corporation and key elements within it perceive and respond to different pressures and opportunities. These cultures and values can be shaped by corporate leaders, by codifying their image of the corporate culture in mission statements, codes of conduct and so on. Indeed, Schoenberger (2000) argues that the shaping of corporate cultures (by accepting some forms of change and rejecting others) is a demonstration of the leaders' power. It is also important to acknowledge that some aspects of the corporate culture may be beyond the reach of senior leaders, being shaped by history, the values of employees and the prevalence and resilience of different sub-cultures within the organisation (Schein, 2010).

Interactions between external and internal forms of governance

Of course, we can expect different forms of external and internal governance to interact and to co-evolve in various ways. One form of external governance is likely to influence another, for example when governments mandate access to information that then enables different forms of market or social pressure to be applied (Gouldson, 2004). Furthermore, different forms of external governance might have a greater impact when they align and resonate with one another – as could be expected where business leaders and NGOs form coalitions of interest (e.g. to lobby for strong international climate change policy) or when consumer interest in adopting energy-saving measures is reinforced by high energy prices or media attention on climate change (see Egels-Zanden and Hyllman, 2006).

External governance interventions can also influence internal governance processes. One example could be where requirements for the disclosure of information on performance render previously private issues such as the behaviour of a person or a firm amenable to external scrutiny and influence; a case in point might be the role that corporate disclosures play in enabling investors to hold them to account for their social and environmental performance (Sullivan, 2011a; Sullivan and Gouldson, 2012). Another example could be where external governance pressures such as government policy or investor pressure encourage the take-up of particular forms of internal corporate governance.

Conversely, internal governance conditions can conspire to shape external governance conditions – for example, when the social values of employees change the ways in which a company behaves (Hemingway, 2005), when corporate cultures alter the ways in which a firm engages with its stakeholders (Andriof, 2002) or when business engagement with government influences the shape, form or direction of policy (Bouwen, 2004).

Finally, we might expect external governance forces to be mediated through a range of internal conditions before they have an effect, for example as social pressures for corporate responsibility are detected, articulated and amplified or attenuated in different firms in different ways depending on the governance conditions within firms. This raises the prospect that different governance pressures may have the greatest impact where they align with each other and where they somehow resonate with or are amplified by receptive conditions within the individual or organisation that is the target of the governance intervention.

Understanding the interaction between different governance forms

The preceding discussion distinguishes between 'governance from the outside' (i.e. where public, private and civic actors engage in activities that seek to shape the behaviour or performance of an individual or organisation) and 'governance from the inside' (i.e. where behaviour is shaped by, for example, the structures and systems, resources and opportunities and cultures and values of organisations). It also highlights the potential for external and internal governance processes to interact in different ways, emphasising that governance interventions may have the greatest influence where different external governance pressures align with each other, where they somehow resonate with or are amplified by receptive conditions within the individual or organisation that is the target of the governance intervention.

Such arguments can be simplified or abstracted further to consider the governance conditions under which changes in corporate behaviour or performance are most likely. With a focus on the governance of corporations, we suggest here that the ability of a particular set of governance conditions to change the behaviour or performance of a business will be shaped by the strength and alignment of the range of external governance pressures surrounding the business on the one hand, and by the strength and alignment of the internal governance conditions within that business on the other. We define strength as the relative power and influence of a particular intervention or framework, and alignment as the level of resonance or synergy between different interventions or frameworks.

In Figure 3.1, we propose a simple framework that can be used to examine the validity of this hypothesis. By distinguishing between strong and well-aligned and weak and poorly aligned governance pressures both around and within the business, we can identify four distinct sets of governance conditions.

Collective action

Where strong and well-aligned external governance pressures meet with similarly strong and well-aligned internal or corporate governance conditions, collective action is the most likely result. We can define collective action as a situation where public, private, civic and other actors are working together or, more generally, where each is taking actions that reinforces and supports the actions of others, and where these actions align with what business sees as its own interests. Such conditions could be realised, for example, where a business is the target of multiple pressures from different sources that are all pushing for

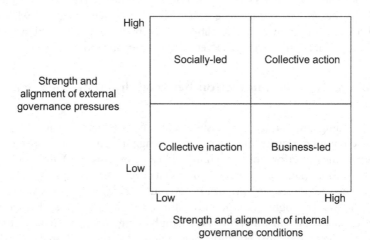

Figure 3.1 Interactions between external governance pressures and internal governance conditions

(adapted from Gouldson and Sullivan, 2014)

a particular type of change in its behaviour, and where that business is willing to change as the pressures somehow resonate with its culture and values; where there are appropriate structures, systems and resources in place to deliver change; and where it recognises an opportunity or some benefit from changing.

Collective inaction

Conversely, when both external pressures and internal conditions are weak or are not well aligned, collective inaction is more likely to occur. We can define collective inaction as a situation where public, private, civic and other actors are not working together or, more generally, where each is taking actions that conflict with the actions of others, and where business does not see that its interests are well served by taking action or responding positively to these pressures. Conditions such as these might occur when a business encounters a range of external pressures that are weak or contradictory, and when that business is either unwilling to respond because its cultures and values render it unreceptive, because it lacks the structures, systems and resources needed to respond or because it does not recognise any opportunity or benefit from changing.

Socially led governance

Where external pressures are strong and are well aligned, but internal conditions are weak or are poorly aligned, socially led governance based on social pressures that are either ignored, resisted or partially accepted by business is the most likely outcome. We can define socially led governance as a situation where public, private, civic and other actors are working together or, more generally, where each is taking actions that reinforce and support the actions of others, but where business sees that its interests are not best served by taking action or responding positively to these external pressures. The outcomes of these governance conditions will depend on whether the social pressure is stronger than any business resistance. These conditions might emerge where a business encounters pressure to change from a range of sources, but is unwilling to respond because the pressures contradict its values. Or it is unable to change because it lacks the systems, structures or resources needed to change or does not see any benefit from changing.

Business-led governance

The mirror image of socially led governance occurs when external governance pressures are weak or are poorly aligned, but where internal governance conditions are strong and are well aligned. Here we predict a phase of business-led governance based on processes of change that are driven by pressures or conditions that emerge from within business, but that are ignored, resisted or partially accepted by social actors. We define business-led governance as a situation where public, private, civic and other actors are not working together or, more generally, where each is taking actions that conflict with the actions of others, and where business sees that its interests are best served by proactively taking action even in the absence of external pressures. The outcomes of these governance conditions depend on whether the self-interest of business is stronger than any social resistance that it might encounter. Such conditions might arise where a business has a strong cultural commitment to a particular form of change, where it has the structures, systems and resources needed to change and/or where it has a strong interest in changing.

Concluding comments

The framework presented in Figure 3.1 presents us with a tool that enables us first to characterise the particular set of governance conditions that exist at a particular point in time, and then to predict their influence, according to the strength and alignment of external governance pressures on the one hand and internal governance conditions on the other. It also allows us to offer practical proposals on how the conditions might change to deliver the specific social or environmental outcomes that are being sought.

The value of the heuristic depends on analysts being able to identify and distinguish between stronger and weaker, and more or less well aligned, governance pressures and conditions both around and within corporations. In Chapters 4 and 5, we use the heuristic to analyse how companies in a specific sector – retail – have responded to the issue of climate change.

4 Governance and corporate action on climate change

The UK supermarket sector

In Chapters 2 and 3 we explored some of the key elements of the governance debate. We examined how public, private and civic actors engage in activities that seek to shape the behaviour or performance of a corporation, how these external governance processes structures might interact with organisations' internal governance (e.g. management systems, organisational resources and capacities, organisational culture and values), and how these interactions might shape corporate behaviour.

Why focus on the UK supermarket sector?

Four factors underpinned our decision to focus on the UK supermarket sector. First, the characteristics of the companies in the sector – significant operational (specifically, building and transport-related) emissions, large supply chain emissions, significant stakeholder and consumer pressure, complex supply chains, relatively little overarching regulation but significant regulation of specific activities – are common to many sectors outside of heavy industry.

Second, the sector is both economically and environmentally significant. In the period covered by our research (2000 to 2015), the UK was one of the world's largest grocery markets (ranked ninth largest in 2011 [IGD, 2012]). The supermarkets headquartered or listed in the UK were among the largest in the world. Based on sales in 2010, Tesco was the third largest retailer in the world, with J Sainsbury (widely referred to as Sainsbury's) ranked 29th, Wm Morrison (or Morrisons) 32nd, Marks and Spencer 55th, the Co-operative Group 69th and the John Lewis Partnership (which included Waitrose) 80th (Deloitte, 2012). The sector's environmental footprint was correspondingly large. In 2008, it was estimated that UK supermarkets' emissions through the use of lighting, heating, cold stores and on-shelf refrigeration accounted for 0.9% of the UK's greenhouse gas emissions, and that emissions from the sector's value and supply chains – for example, agricultural inputs, food manufacture, transport, storage, distribution, refrigeration and packaging, as well as home cooking – are an order of magnitude higher (SDC, 2008: 40).

Third, the sector has a long record of corporate responsibility and climate change-related reporting, which allowed the sector's actions and performance on climate change to be tracked over time. For example, Sainsbury's first reported in 1998 and Waitrose, Tesco and Marks and Spencer first reported in the early 2000s.

Fourth, there was a step change in the sector's focus on climate change from 2006 to 2008, with many of the UK supermarkets making significant policy and financial commitments to both reducing their own greenhouse gas emissions and to working with their suppliers and customers to reduce emissions up and down their value chains. This change was catalysed by a variety of external pressures and incentives, including market conditions, social expectations, media portrayals, customer concerns, voluntary codes, and various economic and information-based policy measures (including the UK Climate Change Levy, Climate Change Agreements and the CRC Scheme). While these external governance pressures were, at least individually, relatively weak, they coincided and coalesced into what was seen as strong external pressure for corporate action on climate change. This confluence and alignment of pressures occurred at a point when UK supermarkets had relatively well-developed internal systems and processes for environmental and energy management, and when many were already constructively engaged in a variety of social and environmental issues. The fact that climate change became such a central issue for so many companies at broadly the same time meant that the UK supermarket sector was an intriguing example of how external governance pressures can drive change, and of the characteristics that determine whether these external pressures will in fact lead to change. Furthermore, the relationship between external governance pressures, internal governance conditions and corporate responses on climate change was far from static over the period 2000 to 2015, allowing us to explore how these evolve and shape each other.

Our research on the UK supermarket sector

Our analysis of the climate change strategies and performance of the UK supermarket sector involved three stages. First, we identified a number of standard performance measures (e.g. total greenhouse gas emissions, energy intensity) that we could use to track the performance of individual companies over time and that we could use to make meaningful comparisons between companies. We then used the data presented in companies' corporate responsibility reports (or equivalent corporate publications) and their responses to the CDP (previously the Carbon Disclosure Project) to analyse trends in absolute and relative greenhouse gas emissions from individual companies and from the sector as a whole.

Second, we conducted a detailed content and data analysis of the information presented in companies' corporate responsibility (or equivalent) reports, annual reports, CDP responses and other published materials covering the period 2000–2015. This enabled us to determine when climate change and energy-related issues appeared on the corporate agenda and to track the evolution of companies' policies, actions and targets on climate change and energy-related issues.

Third, we conducted a series of interviews with the corporate responsibility managers (or equivalent) and other operational managers of Asda, the Co-operative Group, Marks and Spencer, Sainsbury's, Tesco and Waitrose. These interviews focused on issues such as the drivers for corporate action on climate change and energy-related issues, and the manner in which corporate actions and targets have developed over time. We complemented these interviews with interviews with stakeholders – policymakers, NGOs, investors – who had analysed and worked on the sector's approach to climate change.

Our analysis of the UK supermarket sector focused primarily on seven companies: Asda, the Co-operative Group, Marks and Spencer, Sainsbury's, Tesco, Waitrose and Wm Morrison. These companies accounted for well over 80% of the UK grocery market throughout the period covered by this research. However, in particular from 2010 onwards, the German retailers Aldi and Lidl were increasingly significant market actors – in particular from a price perspective – and they accounted for about 10% of the UK grocery market by 2015. We discuss Aldi and Lidl in Chapter 5, as part of our discussion of global retailers.

Governance from the outside: the changing business environment for UK supermarkets

For UK supermarkets, the climate change debate went through three distinct stages: (a) prior to 2005 where climate change was seen as being of lower importance, (b) from 2005 to 2008/2009 where climate change was widely seen as the key environmental issue for the sector, and (c) post 2009 where climate change remained important but some of the pressures for action weakened. We discuss each of these stages in turn.

Prior to 2005

From the late 1990s through to 2005, a variety of issues appeared on – and often subsequently disappeared from – the corporate responsibility agenda of retailers. These included organic food, food miles, responsible sourcing, recycling, ethical trading, sustainable raw materials and animal welfare. Energy management was one of these issues, primarily driven by cost concerns.

Prior to 2005, corporate capacities and resources were allocated to energy management to the extent that there was a financial business case to reduce energy and fuel use. However, apart from the general pressure to reduce costs and save money, it is fair to say that the external pressures for action on climate change were relatively weak; government policies on climate change had yet to impact significantly on the supermarket sector, private pressures (e.g. investor or business-to-business pressures) were not pronounced, and civic pressures (e.g. customer and NGO) were only occasionally influential. The result was that climate change was seen as of secondary importance. When companies did talk about climate change, it was usually in the context of their actions on operational efficiency and/or energy management rather than as a stand-alone issue.

2005–2009

This conception of climate change as a corporate responsibility issue of secondary importance changed dramatically between 2005 and 2007. A number of factors combined to make this a 'tipping point' where climate change not only moved to the heart of the corporate responsibility debate but also started to be recognised as an important part of corporate strategy. Most obviously, there was a growing scientific and public consensus about the importance of climate change as an environmental and economic issue (Sullivan and Pfeifer, 2009). The publication of the fourth Assessment Report of the Intergovernmental Panel on Climate Change (IPCC, 2007), the publication of the Stern Review on the Economics of Climate Change (Stern, 2006) and the 2006 release of Al Gore's film *An Inconvenient Truth* all attracted huge levels of media coverage in the UK. The higher profile of climate change was reflected in consumer surveys. Whereas in its 2003 response to the Carbon Disclosure Project, Marks and Spencer had stated that employment conditions, ethical trading, the responsible use of technology, sustainable raw materials and animal welfare were the major social, ethical and environmental issues that were of concern to its customers, in its 2007 response it stated that it had seen a significant increase in customer awareness and concern about climate change. Similar views were expressed by other retailers (see, for example, Co-operative Group, 2007: 71, 2008: 66). In parallel, the mainstream and business press coverage of climate change changed from positions of apathy or even hostility to the idea that climate change was a business issue to one where there was a reasonably broad acceptance of the scientific predictions and of the need for business to be part of the solution. Climate change moved from the science or environmental pages to the business pages and, perhaps most importantly, was routinely covered in business publications such as the *Financial Times* (Pfeifer and Sullivan, 2008).

Regulation, albeit not directly targeted at the supermarket sector, was also important. The introduction of the EU's Emissions Trading Scheme was seen across the corporate and investment communities as a definitive statement of governments' intent – both within the European Union and beyond – to take action on climate change and to regulate greenhouse gas emissions (Pinske and Kolk, 2009; Pfeifer and Sullivan, 2008; Sullivan, 2008; Sullivan and Pfeifer, 2009). At the same time, electricity and energy prices, in part because of emissions trading (Sullivan and Blyth, 2006) and in part because of wider market forces (e.g. oil prices were above $100 a barrel in 2007), rose significantly.

Finally, peer pressure within the supermarket sector was important. In 2007, Marks and Spencer committed to making its UK and Republic of Ireland operations carbon neutral by 2012 and to working with its customers and suppliers to help reduce their emissions (Marks and Spencer, 2007). Shortly afterwards, Tesco committed to reducing its own carbon footprint and to working with its suppliers and other organisations to deliver significant greenhouse gas emission reductions across the supply chain (Leahy, 2007). Other retailers – and, to the chagrin of at least some of our interviewees, not only those that were recognised as corporate responsibility leaders – started to aggressively market their social and environmental credentials. The 2007 John Lewis Partnership CSR report commented that '...the last year has seen a flurry of CSR activity in the retail industry, as many companies have sought to champion their green credentials to customers and others' (John Lewis Partnership, 2007: 1). In its 2007 Sustainability Report, the Co-operative Group pointed to the dramatic increase in the range of business sectors attracting attention for their environmental performance, noting that the food retail sector in particular had started to aggressively compete on the basis of environmental performance and had initiated a range of commitments and targets to reduce environmental impact (Co-operative Group, 2007).

The pressure on companies to take action on climate change remained strong through 2008 and 2009, with the UK government's adoption of mandatory carbon reduction targets, the strong prospect of an international agreement on climate change, ongoing media coverage and NGO campaigns all combining to keep climate change high on the corporate agenda.

Post 2009

Certain of these pressures weakened between 2009 and 2013. The failure of the 2009 Copenhagen Conference of the Parties to the United Nations Framework Convention on Climate Change to negotiate a successor treaty to the Kyoto Protocol suggested that international efforts on climate change were stalling. The tone of media coverage turned somewhat more hostile, with controversies about the science of climate change (notably the Climategate scandal [see BBC, 2019]) receiving extensive media coverage. Economic and competitiveness concerns in the wake of the 2008 global financial crisis also meant that politicians were vocal in support of strong policy action on climate change.

While company interviewees commented that it was not clear that the UK government would continue to support strong targets in the absence of an international agreement on climate change, the UK continued to develop and implement policy through this period. Those that were of direct relevance to the supermarket sector included the UK Climate Change Levy (which encouraged companies to reduce their energy consumption or use energy from renewables through imposing a tax on electricity, gas and solid fuel usage), Climate Change Agreements (where participating firms received significant reductions in their Climate Change Levy payments in return for meeting energy-saving or carbon reduction targets), and the CRC Scheme (where companies were required to monitor and report on their energy usage and to offset their emissions). In addition, under the 2008 Climate Change Act, the UK committed to reduce emissions by at least 100% of 1990 levels (net zero) by 2050 and to contribute to global emission reductions, to limit global temperature rise to as little as possible above 2°C. To meet these targets, the UK government set five-yearly carbon budgets which restricted the amount of greenhouse gases the UK could legally emit in each five-year period.

Governance from the inside: systems and processes, values and beliefs, costs and benefits

The manner in which the UK supermarkets responded to these external pressures was influenced by their internal management infrastructure, including their formal management systems, by their organisational capacity and expertise and by organisational attitudes and beliefs, in particular views on the business relevance of climate change and the business case for action.

Management systems and processes

In the late 1990s and early 2000s, the companies in the supermarket sector started to professionalise their approach to the management of their environmental and social (or corporate responsibility) issues. They adopted environmental or sustainability policies, allocated board and senior management responsibilities for corporate responsibility issues, established management systems to identify, assess and manage environmental issues, and started to report on their environmental (and, subsequently, social performance).

Sainsbury's issued its first environmental report in 1998, Waitrose, Tesco and Marks and Spencer first reported in the early 2000s, and Asda, the Co-operative Group and Morrisons had all issued corporate responsibility reports by the mid-2000s. All seven continued to publish comprehensive annual corporate responsibility or sustainability reports, with five (the exceptions were the John Lewis Partnership, and the Co-operative Group, neither of whom were publicly listed companies) also reporting to the CDP (previously the Carbon Disclosure Project). Within this reporting, there was a clear move away from the qualitative reporting that characterised earlier reports. From the mid-2000s onwards, the supermarkets started to provide more quantitative data, including information on trends in their performance and on their performance against their targets. While we do not cover them explicitly in this chapter, both Aldi and Lidl were exceptions to this trend towards greater transparency, providing little information on their approach to energy management and climate change, even as late as 2015. This relative lack of disclosure reflected their market positions as discount retailers, and some of the specific characteristics of the German retail market (which we discuss in more detail in Chapter 5).

Within this wider trend towards formalising corporate responsibility management systems and reporting, there was a clear change in the emphasis placed on climate change and energy management. From the late 1990s through to the early to mid-2000s, climate change was presented as being of secondary importance, and was usually presented as part of the company's actions on operational efficiency and/or energy management. This changed from the mid-2000s, with climate change being presented as a central element of each company's corporate environmental strategies, and with corporate responsibility reports providing extensive descriptions of each organisation's governance and management structures for climate change, their climate change policies, their objectives and targets, and the actions taken and outcomes achieved.

This change in priority was reflected in the level of senior management attention focused on climate change. Around the mid-2000s, the supermarkets started to establish board-level committees on corporate responsibility and/or assign overarching responsibility for corporate responsibility to a named board member (usually the CEO) or senior manager. Many of the company interviewees pointed to the importance of leadership, noting that these leaders – and the issues they identified as important – played a key role in creating the cultures and defining the priorities that governed the day-to-day realities of how they did business.

Internal capacity and governance

One of the key themes that emerged from our interviews with the UK retailers was that formal systems and processes for managing greenhouse gas emissions and energy usage were critical to enable them to respond effectively to external pressures and to deliver on their own corporate policies. Within this, the setting of targets – and the associated processes of assigning responsibilities for the delivery of these targets, the allocation of financial and other resources for the delivery of these targets, the monitoring of performance against these targets, internal and external reporting – were consistently highlighted as the mechanism used to translate high-level corporate commitments and policies into tangible action.

Interviewees also highlighted the contribution that climate change and energy-related targets make to developing organisational capacities on climate change. This is well illustrated by the supermarkets' approach to innovation. All of the supermarkets had – from climate change, energy and cost-saving perspectives – an explicit focus on developing more efficient stores and buildings, and on improving the efficiency of their transportation and logistics-related activities. The interviewees explained that, when they and their company made investment decisions, their options reflected the technologies that are available and their own internal knowledge, skills and capacities. One of the key strategies of all of the UK supermarkets was to test energy efficiency and other technologies in 'green stores' or in 'flagship' projects, with the aim of rolling out cost-effective innovations across their business. Similarly, on transport, a number of the retailers worked with engine and vehicle manufacturers to test new technologies (e.g. electric vehicles, biofuels). What was striking was not that the supermarkets were involved in these sorts of projects (as many companies had similar initiatives) but how the retailers used their target-setting processes to ensure that cost-effective innovations were deployed across the entire business. In addition to headline targets on energy efficiency and greenhouse gas emissions, they all had targets – some public, some internal – relating to the development of green stores and to the testing of green technologies. They also had targets relating to the wider deployment of cost-effective technologies and approaches across their business, including requirements that new technologies were integrated into store refurbishment and upgrade processes. Interviewees explained this meant that even if the pace of testing new technologies slowed, the average efficiency of stores would continue to improve for a number of years as stores were progressively refurbished or upgraded. They also noted that this approach to technology test-ing and deployment reflected one of the competitive advantages of large retailers; the size and scale of major retailers meant that, if they identified a cost-effective technology or approach, they had large numbers of buildings and vehicles across which these new technologies could be deployed. Due to economies of scale and through learning by doing, the costs per building or per vehicle basis were fre-quently relatively modest.

The benefits of setting and delivering greenhouse gas and energy-related targets provided a range of benefits to the supermarkets. Reducing greenhouse gas emissions and saving energy enabled them to reduce their costs and improve efficiency and demonstrate their commitment to action on climate change. From a climate change perspective, a number of interviewees reflected that the success of their efforts to reduce their own greenhouse gas emissions had given them the confidence to focus effort on reducing emissions from their supply chains. They also commented that their success in reducing their own costs meant that senior managers were more supportive of further efforts to reduce emissions, and were more open to the idea that the company should engage with its customers and suppliers on these issues.

The business (financial) case for action

One of the central findings from our interviews was that most of the actions that had been taken by the UK supermarkets on climate change (in particular, those that involved large capital investment or significant organisational resources) could be explained simply by considering the financial costs and benefits of the actions taken. We identified relatively few cases where the actions taken were not underpinned by a reasonably robust financial case for action. This does not mean that companies did not realise other benefits from these actions (e.g. PR benefits from badging energy-saving programmes as climate change initiatives). Rather, these benefits were frequently seen as ancillary to the primary driver for action. This focus on cost savings and financial returns reflected – and continues to reflect – a fundamental characteristic of the supermarket sector: it is highly cost competitive and marginal changes in the sales price of particular items can have a huge impact on the profitability of that product.

When we discussed this in more detail with interviewees, we found that all of the supermarkets expected their energy and climate change-related invest-ments to deliver relatively short payback periods; two- or three-year payback periods were very much the norm. These expectations were the same as the rates of return expected of other capital investments. That is, energy efficiency and greenhouse gas emission reduction-related expenditures were not priori-tised over other capital investments. Interviewees did, however, point to the benefits of having longer-term as well as shorter-term climate change and energy-related targets. They noted that having longer-term targets allowed capital investments to be much better aligned with business investment cycles. For example, returning to the innovation example discussed above, longer-term targets meant that investments in store efficiency could be carried out at the point when other upgrades or refurbishments were being scheduled, thereby minimising business disruption and enabling the overall costs (for energy efficiency and upgrades) to be minimised.

UK supermarkets seemed to adopt two distinct approaches to setting climate change and energy-related targets. Some started by conducting a detailed cost-benefit assessment of the options available to them, and then setting targets based on what they thought could be achieved in a cost-effective manner. Others set, often somewhat arbitrarily, targets and then challenged the relevant managers to work out how these would be achieved. Interviewees from these companies indicated that, while a comprehensive business case analysis may not have underpinned the overall commitments, individual projects and investments continued to be subject to normal cost-benefit assessments and were expected to provide reasonable rates of return. That is, the commitments were not seen as commitments that had to be achieved at all costs; rather, they were seen as commitments that would be delivered if there was also a robust business case for action. This is a critically important point – when responding to the wider range of governance pressures, corporate leaders can make bold rhetorical statements or adopt ambitious targets knowing that other corporate governance structures are in place that will ensure that only measures supported by a strong business case will actually be adopted.

In conclusion, the evidence from the UK supermarkets is that actions that were driven by cost pressures or where there was a clear business case for action had a high degree of dependability, as these actions aligned with the general business pressures to be more efficient. In the specific case of climate change, this meant that so long as energy prices remained high and/or there was a meaningful price attributed to greenhouse gas emissions, the retailers would continue to see a compelling argument to maintain their focus on improving their energy efficiency and reducing their greenhouse gas emissions.

Corporate responses: past, present and future

Between 2000 and 2015, the UK supermarkets took action to reduce greenhouse gas emissions from their buildings, transport fleets and supply chains. They also set objectives and targets that provided a clear indication of how they expected their greenhouse gas emissions and energy consumption to change over time. In this section we analyse the actions taken by the UK supermarkets, the performance outcomes they achieved and those they expected to achieve in the future.

Reducing energy and emissions from buildings and transport

From the late 1990s/early 2000s, improving energy efficiency and reducing greenhouse gas emissions from operations and transport was a major area of focus for the supermarket sector. They adopted new energy monitoring and control systems, installed energy-efficient lighting, refrigeration, heating and ventilation equipment in buildings, required new buildings to be more energy efficient and introduced more efficient vehicles into their transport fleets (see, generally, British Retail Consortium, 2009, 2010, 2012, 2013, 2014). They also reduced their non-energy related greenhouse gas emissions (with refrigeration being a major focus). A number made explicit commitments to purchase renewable electricity and/or generate their own electricity using renewable sources. For example, prior to 2007, the John Lewis Partnership derived over 40% of its annual electricity from renewable sources but, from October 2007, all of the company's electricity was obtained from certified green sources (John Lewis Partnership, 2007: 3, 2010: 29, 2014: 33). Similarly, since 2005, virtually all of the electricity supplied to the Co-operative Group was sourced from good-quality renewable sources (wind, hydro and biomass) (Co-operative Group, 2006: 23, 2007: 74, 2009: 67, 2013b: 50).

The effect of these efforts on greenhouse gas emissions from the UK super-markets is summarised in Table 4.1. The data show that the supermarkets consistently improved their greenhouse gas emissions and energy intensity over time. The rate of improvement in energy and greenhouse gas emissions inten-sity compared favourably to the annual improvements in UK economy-wide energy intensity (measured in energy intensity per unit of GDP) of 2.3% per annum between 2005 and 2010 and 2.1% between 1990 and 2010 (European Environment Agency, 2013).

One of the most important conclusions from our interviews was that there was no 'silver bullet'. The consistent year-on-year improvements in energy efficiency that each company achieved were best understood as the outcome from a range of disparate activities and actions directed at reducing energy use and greenhouse gas emissions. This was a recurring theme in corporate responsibility reports across the period 2000 to 2015. Companies explained that their actions on climate change encompassed a whole series of actions including training, installing new control systems, investing in energy-efficient equipment and so forth. Even the Co-operative Group, which reported the largest reductions in its total greenhouse gas emissions, attributed these changes to a mix of behavioural change, refrigerant leak reduction, the installation of new equipment (e.g. replacing old lights with LEDS), retrofitting equipment and capital investments in new stores (Co-operative Group, 2011b: 51).

From a climate change perspective, the more important question is whether efficiency gains will run ahead of business growth and business changes over the longer term (or, as discussed by Dyllick and Hockerts [2002], whether eco-efficiency is the same as eco-effectiveness). For the seven companies, where it is possible to assess performance over at least five years, the evidence is mixed (again, see Table 4.1). Four of the seven succeeded in reducing their absolute greenhouse gas emissions but three saw their emissions increase. The overall effect was that the total greenhouse gas emissions from the UK supermarket sector reduced by approximately 1.1% per year over a period of five to seven years. Various factors influenced these performance outcomes. All of the supermarkets were explicitly focused on growth, not only in financial terms such as profit and turnover but also in terms of market share, the number of stores, and the number of countries of operation. Structural changes also affected greenhouse gas emissions. From 2000 the changes seen in the UK supermarket sector included extended opening hours, the introduction of online shopping and home deliveries, which increased the retailers' transport-related emissions, and customer demand for more fresh foods, which increased the need for in-store refrigeration. These changes all exerted upward pressure on the supermarkets' emissions, although certain of the changes (e.g. internet shopping) may have reduced emissions elsewhere.

Reducing supply chain and value chain-related emissions

Environmental issues, such as climate change, were widely seen by the UK supermarkets as a way of engaging and developing better relationships with their customers, as a means of enhancing their brand and reputation, and as a way of selling more environmental or 'green' products to these customers. From 2005 onwards, the supermarkets all started to provide their customers with information about the environmental/climate change characteristics of their products (e.g. product labelling), with guidance on environmentally responsible behaviour (e.g. encouraging lower temperature washing), and with incentives to purchase green products. While these were all seen as positive contributions, a number of interviewees commented that efforts were focused on supporting relatively minor changes in purchasing decisions, rather than more fundamentally altering patterns of consumption or encouraging less consumption.

The retailers also invested significant time and resource in reducing supplier-related greenhouse gas emissions. Asda, the Co-operative Group, Marks and Spencer, Morrisons, Sainsbury's, Tesco and Waitrose all established programmes to help suppliers improve their environmental performance and/or meet minimum environmental standards, with agricultural products being a major focus in this regard (see, for example, Co-operative Group, 2013b: 53; John Lewis Partnership, 2012: 54; Tesco, 2014a: 28; Wm Morrison, 2013: 24). The support provided included environmental guides, IT tools and the sharing of best practices. Reducing greenhouse gas emissions was a particular area of focus. For example, Sainsbury's reported that its Dairy Development Group's carbon-footprinting tool enabled farmers to reduce their energy costs and carbon footprints by approximately 10% (J Sainsbury 2008: 11, 2010: 25), Morrisons worked with universities to research renewable energy options to help cut electricity usage and costs on dairy farms, and Asda worked with a number of its fresh food (eggs, milk, potatoes, lamb and chicken) suppliers to map the embedded carbon in their products.

These efforts were not motivated by altruism. In part they were motivated by the desire to reduce supplier energy consumption and, hence, product costs. They were also motivated by the need to ensure the sustainability of agriculture supply chains, both to ensure that suppliers were able to stay in business and to ensure that suppliers did not defect to other retailers. The supermarkets recognised the cost reduction pressures they had put on their suppliers over many years, and recognised that they needed to somewhat redress the balance through offering better terms (prices, duration of contracts), working with suppliers to help them to improve their performance and efficiency, and preferentially purchasing from suppliers with better environmental performance. These arguments should be taken with a pinch of salt, given that the supermarkets expected to at least share, if not capture most of, the financial benefits of reduced energy costs. Furthermore, supermarkets' purchasing departments were still charged with extracting as many cost savings as possible from their suppliers.

Objectives and targets

Within modern corporations, targets are the point at which corporate policies are translated into action and where resources are allocated. They also provide important insights into corporate priorities, corporate strategy and how the company sees its future.

The manner in which the companies in the UK supermarket sector defined their climate change-related targets changed significantly over the period 2000 to 2015. They changed from process to performance targets, moved from relative to absolute targets, lengthened the timeframe over which their targets apply and broadened the scope of their targets by increasing the emphasis on supply chain and value chain-related issues.

Up to the mid-2000s, supermarkets' climate change and energy-related targets were primarily process-focused – a typical example was to investigate a specific energy-saving technology – and short term (e.g. over the next 12 months) in nature. Where targets related to performance, they were generally defined in relative terms (e.g. to improve the proportion of vehicle fleets meeting a certain efficiency standard, to improve building efficiency, to reduce energy consumption per unit of floor area).

Around the mid-2000s, the retailers started to publish much more precise targets, focusing on specific emission reductions and performance improvements. An increasing number of targets were set over three or five years, rather than one year, although they continued to focus on relative rather than absolute performance. Typical examples were to reduce greenhouse gas emissions per unit of stock transported, to reduce greenhouse gas emissions per unit of floor area, and to build new stores that were more efficient than equivalent existing stores. These targets were often supplemented by shorter-term targets focusing on improved management processes and controls, with a particular focus on introducing new monitoring and control systems. These supplementary targets allowed for closer control of operating performance, while also generating data that could be used in corporate responsibility reports.

Since 2007, following the lead set by Marks and Spencer and Tesco, the UK supermarkets progressively set more ambitious and longer-term targets for their operations and activities. Table 4.2 summarises the major greenhouse gas-related commitments that had been set by the UK supermarkets as at June 2014. These commitments were underpinned by shorter-term targets, comprising a mix of process, relative and absolute targets (the relative and absolute targets are presented in Tables 4.3 and 4.4). These targets applied over a range of timeframes, and to operations, supply chains and value chains. The retailers committed significant resources to low-carbon and related investments. For example, Tesco committed to spending £500 million between 2007 and 2012 on low-carbon technologies to reduce its emissions (Tesco, 2007: 25), the Co-operative Group committed to doubling its financial support for renewable energy and energy efficiency projects from £400 million to £1 billion by 2013 (Co-operative Group, 2011a: 9) and Marks and Spencer estimated that Plan A would cost it £200 million between 2007 and 2012 (Marks and Spencer, 2007: 7).

Many of the targets represented a significant acceleration in the rate at which the supermarkets were reducing their greenhouse gas emissions and improving their energy efficiency, equating to annual absolute greenhouse gas emission reductions of over 2% per annum for some companies, and emissions intensity improvements of 3–7% per annum. Many of the company interviewees were quite confident that they could achieve, if not exceed, their efficiency-related targets. They pointed to their processes for testing and deploying new technologies and new approaches to energy efficiency as giving them a high degree of visibility on the rate of adoption of these new technologies and of the emission reductions or energy savings that they could expect to achieve. They also noted that these long-term targets were broadly in line with the sort of absolute and efficiency improvements that they had previously achieved, giving them the confidence that they could achieve similar gains in forthcoming years. This is supported by the analysis in Table 4.3 of the progress that companies had made against the targets that they had set for themselves.

The high rate of target delivery may, alternatively, suggest that companies were not being as ambitious as they might, and that they were essentially setting targets that they were confident of meeting. This point was acknowledged by a number of company interviewees who expressed concern about the potential for negative press coverage if they failed to meet their climate change targets, no matter how demanding these targets are or how much progress had been made. They explained that this made them wary of making public commitments that were so challenging that it was almost certain they would not be met.

It is important not to forget that, as indicated in Table 4.4, the majority of the sector's targets continued to relate to operations rather than wider supply chain or customer-related emissions. That is, the sector continued to focus most effort on a narrow part of its carbon footprint. The general absence of formal targets for supply chain and value chain-related emissions also reflected the reality that the quantification of and reporting on these emissions was – and continues to be – in its infancy.

Finally, many of the targets being set by the supermarkets were expressed in relative rather than absolute terms. That is, the goal was to improve energy efficiency and/or greenhouse gas emissions intensity, rather than necessarily to reduce absolute greenhouse gas emissions. Interviewees acknowledged this problem, commenting that total greenhouse gas emissions would depend not only on the effectiveness of their efforts to improve energy efficiency and/or greenhouse gas emissions intensity but also on the rate of business growth and the characteristics of this growth.

The interactions between external governance pressures, internal governance and corporate responses

External governance pressures, internal governance conditions and corporate responses on climate change are dynamic; all three evolve over time and the changes in each impact on and influence the others. The UK supermarket case-study provides important insights into how external governance pressures can influence corporate actions and responses, and the factors that determine whether these pressures are more or less likely to influence corporate practice. It also provides important insights into how internal governance conditions and corporate responses influence external governance pressures, and determine the actors likely to exert pressure and the strategies that are likely to be used to exert pressure.

From external governance pressures to corporate responses

External governance pressures and internal governance conditions followed a similar trajectory in the period 2000 to 2015. External governance pressures were relatively weak prior to 2005, strengthened rapidly from 2005 to 2007, remained relatively strong through to 2009, but weakened thereafter.

Internal governance processes were relatively weak prior to 2005; the UK supermarkets had developed some of the capacities and resources they needed to effectively manage their greenhouse gas emissions and energy use, with these being drawn upon to the extent that there were commercial reasons to take some action to reduce their energy and fuel use. From 2006 to 2009, the supermarkets strengthened their internal governance processes. They set climate change-related targets, adopted a rhetoric that empowered their managers to take action, and strengthened their monitoring and management processes. They maintained their focus on climate change and energy efficiency and their organisational capacity and expertise, even as some of the external pressures for action weakened post 2009.

The fact that external governance pressures and internal governance processes developed at broadly the same time across the sector as a whole means that, in the period after 2005, we are dealing with a case where external pressures were acting on entities that understood the issue in question (in this case, climate change), that had established the systems and processes that they needed to manage and monitor their responses to these pressures, and that had the capacity and expertise to respond to these pressures. What is noteworthy is that the external governance pressures on the supermarket sector were, in fact, relatively weak. Notwithstanding the high profile of climate change in the media and as a focus for policy action, the supermarkets faced relatively little direct pressure to take action. Customer pressure (which we discuss further below) was muted, energy prices were a relatively small part of retailers' cost bases, media attention focused on large industrial sources (in particular, the electricity sector and the traditional 'heavy industries'), and there was limited direct regulation of the sector as a whole (although the sector, as with others, did have to meet new equipment, vehicle and building standards). While the individual external governance pressures were relatively weak, they were at least aligned. When discussing the reasons why their company decided to take action on climate change, interviewees explained that the aggregate pressures that they faced at this time convinced them that they needed to take action. While individual interviewees pointed to different pressures as being of greater or lesser importance to their company, there was consensus that the external pressures would be 'long-lasting' and 'only going in one direction', and that it was 'inevitable' that the supermarkets would need to take substantive action on climate change. This perception was reinforced by Tesco and Marks and Spencer's climate change announcements in 2007, and the competition for leadership on the climate change agenda. The companies and stakeholders that we interviewed all noted that climate change rapidly became a defining issue for the sector and that none of the supermarkets could afford to be seen as a laggard.

The other notable finding from the analysis of the UK supermarket sector, and one that applies across the entire period from 2000 to 2015, is the central role played by financial factors in business decision-making. As discussed above, the supermarkets only invested capital in situations when there was a clear financial case for investment, i.e. where the benefits outweighed the costs, when the rate of return met or exceeded the company's investment requirements. If this was the primary finding from this research, it would suggest that corporate action on climate change is solely contingent on market incentives through energy or carbon prices, and/or on government's willingness to mandate or require companies to take particular actions. However, the research suggests that other external governance pressures have a hugely important role to play, even when the business case for action is relatively modest. These governance pressures can encourage companies to develop their internal governance processes and capabilities. As we have seen, these can be institutionalised through the setting of targets, public reporting and structured innovation processes. This institutionalisation means that companies are likely to continue to take at least some action even if the market or regulatory incentives are weak, or if these incentives weaken over time. External governance pressures can also result in companies broadening the scope of action, which again is something we have seen in the UK with many of the supermarkets setting long-term targets (i.e. extending the temporal scope) and looking for emission reduction opportunities in their supply chains and value chains.

Where are the stakeholders?

One of the most interesting findings from the research into the UK super-market sector was the apparently limited influence of external stakeholders on supermarkets' climate change strategies. For example, customers appeared to have paid little attention to the retailers' climate change strategies, investors had not subjected corporate climate change strategies to detailed analysis and, as noted above, the media had paid relatively little attention to the retail sector. When we dig into the reasons for this, we see that there are various factors at play: climate change was just one of many issues of concern to stakeholders; many stakeholders lacked the capacity to exert influence; those stakeholders with the ability to exert influence did not exert their influence effectively; accountability processes did not work effectively. In addition, company responses – their management systems and processes, the actions they had taken, their communications – enabled them to deflect certain external pres-sures and to weaken others. We analyse these themes in more detail by looking at three important stakeholder groups: customers, investors and NGOs.

Consumers

For consumers, climate change was just one of a whole series of issues of concern to them. Far from social or environmental issues being dominant influences, factors such as price, quality, service, product availability and store location were widely seen as much more important determinants of whether or not a customer would decide to shop at a particular retailer. Moreover, the corporate responsi-bility issues that were of concern to consumers tended to be strongly influenced by the media and NGO campaigns. For example, from 2002 to 2005, the issues of concern to customers – reflecting the topics that were covered extensively in the media – included being a good employer, ethical trading, responsible use of technology, use of sustainable raw materials, and animal welfare (J Sainsbury, 2003: 13, 2005: 11–12; Marks and Spencer, 2004: 2). In 2007, as we discussed above, climate change (in particular, reducing energy use) and waste started to receive much greater attention (J Sainsbury, 2007: 5; Marks and Spencer, 2008: 2; Waitrose, 2008: 3) whereas in 2009 and 2010, the prominent issues of concern included the carbon impact of suppliers, the nutritional value of food and responsible sourcing (J Sainsbury, 2009: 15; John Lewis Partnership, 2009: 33–34, 2010: 34). In a 2013 survey, Sainsbury's identified its carbon footprint as being the 14th (out of a list of 22) most important corporate responsibility issue to consumers (J Sainsbury, 2013: 9).

The supermarkets, both in the interviews conducted for this research and in their corporate responsibility reports, regularly expressed frustration that con-sumers did not link the environmental issues they were concerned about with the decisions they made on which supermarkets to shop at. They also expressed concern that consumers were rarely able to articulate their concerns in terms that would direct the actions that should be taken by supermarkets. Customers appeared to assume that, in the absence of information to the contrary, the supermarket is doing a reasonable job of managing environmental and related issues. This is reflected in the approaches adopted by UK supermarkets to managing climate change in the period 2000 to 2015. They accepted that, no matter whether it was explicitly demanded or not, consumers expected them to be environmentally responsible, to minimise their operational impacts and – from 2007/2008 onwards – to provide their customers with opportunities to reduce their environmental impacts through, for example, selling lower environmental impact products. It is interesting that the interviewees from the supermarkets were clear that there was a tension between the need to be ahead of consumer expectations (e.g. through having effective climate change-related strategies) but, at the same time, not being too far ahead of their customers or focusing on issues that are not seen as important by their customers.

While there was limited evidence that consumers explicitly differentiated between the supermarkets on the basis of their climate change strategies, all of the supermarkets recognised that their customers would give effect to their preferences and ethical values in the products that they choose, e.g. through choosing more energy-efficient or environmentally friendly products. The UK supermarkets all tried to engage with their customers on climate change, through providing product-related information, steering specific purchasing decisions and wider awareness raising and education. Product labelling was a particular area of focus. In certain areas – notably electrical goods where product labels were widely recognised and understood by consumers, underpinned by regulatory standards, and focused solely on the consumer's energy use – product labels were seen as a very effective tool for directing customer choice. Developing meaningful labelling schemes for other products proved difficult. The retailers, in particular Tesco which by 2010 had footprinted over 500 of its products and labelled 120, including lightbulbs, orange juice, potatoes, washing detergent, milk, kitchen towel and toilet tissue (Tesco 2010: 12), experimented with similar carbon-footprinting or life-cycle assessment tools. Despite these efforts, product labelling was not widely adopted. There were various reasons for this: the high cost of conducting the assessments; high cost of the labelling process; uncertainty around whether customers would actually use the information provided (a number of retailers were concerned that footprint labels might be confusing); complexity of labelling (with the potential that labels need to revised if there are any changes in the supply chain); risk of over-simplification (e.g. how to trade off different environmental variables in a single label); and lack of consistency around reporting. In our interviews, the supermarkets also raised concerns about the willingness of customers to pay more for products with environmentally desirable characteristics. They commented that climate change is just one of a whole series of environmental issues that customers are concerned about, and that the ability (or inability) of consumers to make informed decisions relies on the information being presented in very simple terms (e.g. A–G energy labelling). Interviewees also referred to the issue of trust, explaining that many customers trust their retailers to effectively manage the social and environmental impacts of the products that they are purchasing. That is, the situation that supermarkets found themselves in was one of delegated responsibility, where customers trusted or relied on the supermarket to manage issues such as climate change, rather than the customer himself/herself being required to take responsibility for these decisions.

Non-governmental organisations

When we look at NGOs, we can divide them into two broad categories. The first are those that work closely with the supermarkets to help develop strategic responses to climate change or sustainability challenges more generally. In the period 2000 to 2015, the most prominent of these in the UK were WWF, Forum for the Future and (while not an NGO per se) the Carbon Trust. Their activities included showcasing good/best practice, raising awareness, challenging companies on their approaches to climate change, board and senior management mentoring, providing strategic and technical advice, and helping develop scenarios and future visions for these companies. These NGOs encouraged supermarkets to integrate sustainability issues into their business strategies and to set longer-term targets on climate change and sustainability issues in the round. While it is difficult to assess their exact influence on the decisions taken by the supermarkets, the NGOs interviewed were of the view that they had played an important role, alongside others, in getting companies to make long-term and ambitious commitments to action on climate change. These NGOs saw that proximity to and working with retailers was an integral part of their strategy, and therefore sought to develop constructive relationships based on shared agendas and supportive dialogue. These NGOs recognised that these engagement strategies limited their ability to criticise companies, as they would run the risk of losing their access and influence.

The second category of NGOs are those who campaign on specific issues. The UK saw many such campaigns between 2000 and 2015. The campaigns covered a variety of topics, including animal welfare, sustainable fishing, ethical trading, sustainable products and commodities. These NGOs focused on linking company performance on these issues to the corporate brand and reputation, using naming and shaming and league tables/benchmarking strategies, to leverage change. Some of these campaigns were very effective and delivered real change. From interviews, with NGOs and with companies, two factors seemed common to the most successful campaigns. The first was, perhaps self-evidently, that the campaigns focused on the supermarkets' brand or reputation. The second was that they focused on specific products. Because the supermarkets had professionalised and strengthened their approach to corporate responsibility (not just climate change), they were usually well positioned to respond effectively to product-specific campaigns, and to offer solutions (e.g. alternative products, sourcing from different suppliers) that satisfied the NGOs while not having a particular impact on their costs.

While product-oriented campaigns were common, NGOs did not campaign on wider corporate responsibility (or climate change) related issues. Both the corporate and the NGO interviewees for this research agreed that such campaigns would be difficult to mount and sustain for a variety of reasons: the complexity of the issues; the difficulty of comparing, for example, performance on climate change with performance on water; the risk of endorsing a company for performance on a specific issue (e.g. on climate change) even if that company lags behind on other aspects of performance; the reality that the retailers were doing a reasonable job of managing most of the major sustainability issues that they faced.

Two points warrant some further discussion in this regard: the manner in which corporate rhetoric on climate change affects the ability of NGOs to exert pressure, and the role that has been played by carbon reporting.

In relation to corporate rhetoric on climate change, the supermarkets' positioning of climate change as a corporate priority made it much more difficult for NGOs to campaign effectively. This positioning enabled the supermarkets to move discussion from one of whether or not they should take action on climate change to what it is that they should do, thereby positioning climate change as a technical issue requiring technical expertise, rather than the more general advice and input that NGOs might be able to provide. This framing allowed the supermarkets to push back on NGO demands on the grounds that NGOs, generally, did not have expertise in implementation and did not understand the complexities of the sector. It allowed them, at least in private, to describe NGO campaigns as overly ambitious, and even unrealistic. It also supported a wider argument that it was companies, not NGOs or civil society, that really understood sustainability issues and that had the people and resources required to manage these issues.

The corporate rhetoric on climate change also appeared to have resulted in some capture of the NGOs and their messages. One of the characteristics of the UK debate between 2005 and 2015 was how NGO agendas were presented as being closely aligned with the manner in which companies see their responsibilities and objectives. For example, Tesco stated in a number of CSR reports that NGOs wanted it to show leadership on corporate responsibility issues from climate change to ethical trading, and they expected Tesco to provide clear policies and principles and to communicate transparently and openly (Tesco, 2007: 12, 2010: 56). In 2008/2009, Marks and Spencer surveyed some of the major UK NGOs (Business in the Community, Carbon Trust, Forum for the Future, Oxfam and WWF-UK) about its climate change efforts. One of the most intriguing findings was that the NGOs identified energy efficiency as a particularly important part of Marks and Spencer's Plan A, its flagship corporate responsibility programme (Marks and Spencer, 2009: 40). This conclusion suggests that, through their engagement with companies, NGOs had been captured by ecological modernisation or efficiency perspectives on corporate sustainability and diverted away from focusing on absolute or total greenhouse gas emissions.

When we look at the role played by NGOs, it is relevant to highlight that one of the key governance mechanisms that they supported, namely carbon disclosure, did not appear to have delivered on its promise. From the mid-2000s onwards, NGOs strongly supported carbon disclosure processes such as the CDP, seeing these as mechanisms that could be used to enhance corporate transparency and accountability and, in turn, drive down greenhouse gas emissions. However, practice has proven quite different. Companies saw these disclosures as a tool for risk management, allowing them to demonstrate their commitment to action, and to frame the debate on climate change in terms that were most favourable to them. Furthermore, even allowing for this inevitable tendency for companies to present information in a way that presents them in the best possible light, the variations in the scope, coverage and consistency of carbon disclosure and reporting continued to make it very difficult to compare corporate performance either over time or with other companies (see further the discussion of corporate reporting in Appendix 1). Interestingly, the supermarket interviewees also commented that NGOs had paid limited attention to the disclosures that the supermarkets did provide (either in their own corporate responsibility reports or to the CDP). They, perhaps cynically, commented that NGOs were happy to call for more disclosure but had limited idea of how they might use or interpret those disclosures that were provided. They also noted that the fact that NGOs did not use these disclosures provided further confirmation of the lack of technical knowledge within NGOs. These findings – that companies appropriated disclosure mechanisms for their own purposes, that it was difficult to use the disclosures to assess performance, and that NGOs did not engage with the disclosures that were provided – suggest that the confidence that NGOs placed in corporate disclosure as meaningful corporate accountability mechanism was not justified. It led to a reality whereby corporate leaders could continue to make strong commitments on climate change and bold statements on carbon performance confident that it would be very difficult to hold them to account, and that it was unlikely that NGOs would even attempt to do so.

Finally, the wider framing of climate change has affected NGOs' ability to hold companies to account. In parallel to the gradual weakening of external governance pressures that have been seen since 2009, the UK supermarkets started to link climate change to wider sustainability-related issues, and to reintegrate climate change back into their broader approach to corporate responsibility; that is, the effect was to make climate change a less explicit priority. There was a practical logic to this; companies need to balance different aspects of their operations, and progress in one area is often accompanied by negative impacts in another. However, the framing of the corporate narrative into one about around the interlinked nature of sustainability challenges also enabled the supermarkets to push back on NGO demands for further action on climate change, on the grounds that taking further action would have overall negative effects. This reframing became more apparent in the latter half of 2014 when reductions in UK electricity and energy prices weakened the business case for action, making certain investments less economically attractive than had previously been the case.

Investors

Investors were identified by the interviewees from the publicly listed super-markets as an important stakeholder. From the mid-2000s, investors encouraged companies to strengthen their climate change-related disclosures, and encouraged publicly listed companies to report to the CDP. Investors also asked companies questions about the financial risks and opportunities presented by climate change, and indicated that they expected companies to have effective management systems and processes in place to manage these risks and opportunities.

While the companies indicated that they had responded positively to these suggestions, it is difficult to attribute substantive impacts on corporate strategies to this engagement. In part, it is because the issues raised by investors tended to mirror those raised by other stakeholders and in the media and so, in some ways, they were just amplifying and reflecting wider societal agendas. In part it was because energy costs were a relatively modest part of the supermarkets' overall cost bases and so retailers were of the view that these were unlikely to be considered financially material by investors (for a discussion of financial materiality as an investment concept, see Sullivan, 2011a).

While investors' influence appeared to have been modest, a number of those interviewed stated that it was important that they were in a position to respond to investor queries and that they were able to demonstrate that their performance compared favourably to that of their industry peers. The reasons for this sensitivity were the fact that greenhouse gas emissions ('carbon') is a metric that can be explicitly included in investment models, the fact that carbon can be used as a proxy for energy use and business efficiency, and the relative maturity of carbon reporting, in particular from 2010 onwards, which meant that it was possible for investors to make direct comparisons between companies.

The interaction between external and internal governance conditions

When we look at the evolution of UK supermarket's responses to climate change, we can identify four distinct phases over the period 2000 to 2015, each with different governance characteristics. These are illustrated in Figure 4.1.

In the first phase, from 2000 through to 2005 or 2006, external governance pressures were relatively weak, at least when compared to what they would become later. Government policies on climate change had yet to impact significantly on the supermarket sector, private (e.g. investor or business-to-business) pressures were not pronounced and civic (e.g. customer and NGO) pressures were only occasionally influential. In the absence of substantial external pressures, the levels of alignment between different pressures were not important; the different pressures neither reinforced nor contradicted each other. Within companies, internal governance conditions were developing slowly with companies building some of the capacities and resources that they needed to effectively manage their greenhouse gas emissions and energy use. Energy prices were increasing, and so corporate capacities and resources were

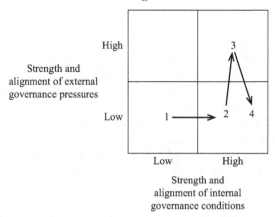

Figure 4.1 Evolving interactions between external and internal governance conditions in the UK supermarket sector (2000–2015)

(Adapted from Gouldson and Sullivan, 2014)

drawn upon to the extent that there were commercial reasons for companies to take some actions to reduce their energy and fuel use. There was a degree of resonance between different internal conditions. We therefore characterise this phase of collective inaction as being equivalent to position 1 in Figure 4.1.

In the second phase, in the short period from 2005 or 2006 to 2007, we see a rapid change in the external pressures for action and, albeit perhaps lagging by a year or two in some cases, companies' internal capacities and resources. Significant external pressures in the form of a stronger scientific consensus that action on climate change was necessary, backed up by the economic case for action presented by the Stern Review, led to rising public concerns, NGO campaigns and media coverage, and a sense that significant and sustained government intervention was inevitable unless business acted. Within the supermarket sector, some chief executives and boards adopted targets and a rhetoric that empowered managers to take action, and other chief executives rapidly followed suit. Capacities to manage energy continued to develop, relatively cash-rich companies had money to invest and energy prices continued to rise so that the business case for investment strengthened. Businesses therefore had strong and well-aligned internal governance conditions that were receptive to the stronger and better-aligned external pressures. The rapid emergence of this set of conditions led to a tipping point in governance arrangements; we characterise this move to business-led governance as being equivalent to a shift from position 1 to position 2 in Figure 4.1.

From 2007 through to 2008 or 2009, external pressures for action gradually strengthened, with the prospect of an international agreement on climate change and the UK government adopting mandatory carbon reduction targets. Social and consumer concern grew, NGOs introduced a number of influential campaigns and media coverage of climate change was high. External pressures were therefore strengthening, and there was a degree of alignment between different pressures that reinforced their significance. Internally, the profile of climate, carbon and energy issues was maintained, with different companies setting broader and more demanding longer-term targets. Capacities for change had continued to develop and viable options for further improvements in energy efficiency were still readily available. With relatively high or volatile energy prices, corporate action was still possible within the constraints of the business case for action, and with low interest rates and relatively buoyant stock markets companies felt confident in investing. We characterise this shift to more collective action as involving a shift from position 2 to position 3. However, even in what would seem to be the most favourable governance conditions, there was little evidence that companies were considering options to substantially reduce their absolute emissions by radically transforming their business models.

Since 2009 or 2010, in particular following the failure at the Copenhagen Conference of the Parties to the United Nations Framework Convention on Climate Change in 2009 to negotiate a successor treaty to the Kyoto Protocol, the governance context changed again. In interviews, company representatives noted that the external pressures encountered by companies were reduced by the failure to reach a global agreement on climate change in 2009 and by controversies around climate science that were amplified by sceptical media coverage. While the impacts of the failure to reach a global agreement on climate change were mitigated by the UK's pre-existing commitments to mandatory carbon reduction targets, recession and the pre-eminence of concerns about competitiveness created a sense that targets may be weakened in time. Public concerns about climate change remained significant, but were competing for attention with shorter-term social and economic concerns. The external governance pressures could, therefore, be described as weakening and as having less coherency or consistency than had previously been the case.

The financial crisis also made companies more reluctant to invest. This was partially offset by energy prices remaining reasonably high and by the continued availability of relatively low-risk options for reducing energy bills. Companies maintained their public commitments, although – as discussed above – these were increasingly integrated with their broader corporate social responsibility initiatives. Internal governance conditions continued to be quite strong and comparatively well aligned. We therefore characterise the period from 2009 to 2015 as a return to business-led governance, involving a shift from position 3 to 4 in Figure 4.1.

Concluding comments

The UK supermarket case-study shows how even weak external governance pressures can – if they are aligned and sustained – result in big changes in corporate practice. Internal governance processes play a critical role in institutionalising these changes and in sustaining progress even when the external pressures weaken or even disappear. However, the evidence is that the actions taken by companies are inevitably constrained by the need for a financial business case that enables the action to be taken. In practice, this means that companies tend to default to incremental changes (e.g. improved energy efficiency) rather than more transformative change of business models.

The case-study also shows that there is a dynamic and interactive relationship between external governance pressures, internal governance conditions and corporate actions. It shows that corporations are responsive to external pressures but that this responsiveness also allows them to influence external pressures, often to weaken or limit the strengthening of the pressures. More importantly, it allows us to understand how this happens and to identify the characteristics of stakeholders and potential accountability mechanisms (e.g. consumer pressures, disclosure requirements) that exacerbate or mitigate these feedback effects.

Supplementary information: UK supermarkets

Table 4.1 Trends in greenhouse gas emissions and energy intensity for UK supermarkets

Company	Annual change in greenhouse gas emissions (%/year)	Annual improvement in energy intensity (%/year)	Annual improvement in greenhouse gas emissions intensity efficiency (%/year)
Asda	−2.98 (over 5 years)		
Co-operative Group	−6.13 (6 years)		
Marks and Spencer	−3.07 (7 years)	+4.32 (7 years)	
Morrisons	−2.56 (7 years)		+3.95 (7 years)
Sainsbury's	+1.43 (7 years)		+4.28 (5 years)
	+1.70 (12 years)	+1.55 (12 years)	
Tesco	+3.03 (7 years)		+4.44 (7 years)
John Lewis Partnership (including Waitrose)	+2.38 (12 years)	+3.82 (8 years)	

Notes:
1 Sources: Asda (2013a, 2013b); Co-operative Group (2013b); J Sainsbury (2004, 2005, 2006, 2007, 2009, 2010, 2011a, 2014); John Lewis Partnership (2009, 2011, 2012, 2014); Marks and Spencer (2014); Tesco (2014a, 2014b); Wm Morrison (2013).
2 Many of the retailers have rebased or restated their emissions or intensity data and, therefore, there are limits to the number of years for which trends can be derived. These data are to 2013 or 2014.

Table 4.2 UK supermarkets' overarching climate change commitments (as at 1 June 2014)

Company	Overarching commitments
Asda	• Reduce Asda's carbon footprint by 10% by 2015 against a 2005 baseline, and continue to reduce Asda's carbon footprint year on year in absolute terms (Asda, 2013a: 2). • Support Walmart's objective to eliminate 20 million tonnes of embedded carbon from its global supply chain by the end of 2015, compared to a 2010 baseline (Asda, 2013a: 3).
Co-operative Group	• Reduce gross greenhouse gas emissions from the Co-operative Group's operations by 50% by 2020, against a 2006 baseline (Co-operative Group, 2013a: 7, 2013b: 48). • Generate the equivalent of 25% of the Co-operative Group's electricity needs from the Co-operative Group's own renewable energy projects by 2017 (Co-operative Group, 2013b: 49).
Marks and Spencer	• Maintain carbon neutrality for Marks and Spencer operated activities in the UK and Republic of Ireland operations until at least 2015 and extend this commitment to include other Marks and Spencer international operations by 2014 (Marks and Spencer, 2014: 26).
Morrisons	• Reduce total operational (electricity, gas, transport, waste, employee work travel, business miles, refrigeration) greenhouse gas emissions by 30% by 2020 against a 2005 baseline (Wm Morrison, 2013: 45).
Sainsbury's	• Reduce operational emissions by 30% in absolute terms and by 65% in relative terms (per unit of floor area) by 2020 compared to a 2005 baseline, as part of a broader target to reduce absolute greenhouse gas emissions by 50% by 2030 (J Sainsbury, 2011b: 9–10, 2013). • Work with Sainsbury's own-brand suppliers to reduce carbon emissions across all of Sainsbury's own-brand products by 50% in relative terms (J Sainsbury, 2011b: 9–10, 2013).
Tesco	• Be a zero-carbon business by 2050 without purchasing offsets (Tesco, 2014a: 28). • Cut supply chain emissions by 30% by 2020 against a 2008 baseline (Tesco, 2013: 39). • Identify ways to help Tesco's customers halve their carbon footprints by 2020 against a 2009 baseline (Tesco, 2013: 39).
John Lewis Partnership (including Waitrose)	• Reduce operational greenhouse gas emissions by 15% by 2020/2021 against a 2010/2011 baseline (John Lewis Partnership, 2014: 33).

Table 4.3 UK supermarkets' specific greenhouse gas emission reduction targets (as at 1 June 2014)

Company	Selected targets	Comments on performance
Asda	• Reduce total greenhouse gas emissions (from energy use, refrigeration, transport, water and travel) by 10% by 2015 against a 2005 baseline (Asda, 2013a: 2).	Asda achieved this target in 2010 and had achieved a 15.8% reduction by the end of 2012 (Asda, 2013a: 3). Asda has committed to continuing to reduce its carbon footprint year on year in absolute terms (Asda, 2013a: 2).
	• Maintain flat energy use for the period 2012 to 2020 (Asda, 2013a: 5).	In the period 2005 to 2012, Asda reduced its store energy use by 33% (Asda, 2013a: 5).
	• Reduce emissions from transport by 60% per case delivered by 2015, versus a 2005 baseline (Asda, 2013a: 5).	Asda achieved a reduction of 47% by the end of 2012 compared to its 2005 baseline (Asda, 2013a: 5).
	• Use 30% renewable energy by 2020 (Asda, 2013a: 5).	Asda reached 3% by the end of 2012 (Asda, 2013a: 5).
	• Achieve an 8% refrigerant leakage rate (Asda, 2013a: 5).	Asda reduced its refrigerant leakage rate from 20% to 7.1% over the period 2005 to 2012 (Asda, 2013a: 5).
Co-operative Group	• Reduce gross greenhouse gas emissions from the Co-operative Group's operations by 50% by 2020, against a 2006 baseline (Co-operative Group, 2013a: 7, 2013b: 48).	The Co-operative Group reduced its gross greenhouse gas emissions by 43% over the period 2006 to 2012 (Co-operative Group, 2013b: 48).
	• Generate the equivalent of 25% of the Co-operative Group's electricity needs from the Co-operative Group's own renewable energy projects by 2017 (Co-operative Group, 2013a: 7, 2013b: 49).	By the end of 2012, 5% of the Co-operative Group's electricity needs were met from the Co-operative Group's renewable energy projects (Co-operative Group, 2013b: 50). In 2012, 98% of the Co-operative Group's electricity requirements was obtained from good-quality renewable sources (Co-operative Group, 2013b: 50).

Company	Selected targets	Comments on performance
Marks and Spencer	• Improve energy efficiency in UK and Republic of Ireland stores by 35% per square foot by 2015 and by 50% by 2020, against a 2006/2007 baseline (Marks and Spencer, 2014: 27).	In 2013/2014, Marks and Spencer reported that it had achieved a 34% improvement on 2006/2007 (Marks and Spencer, 2014: 27).
	• Improve energy efficiency in international stores, offices and distribution centres outside of the Republic of Ireland stores by 20% by 2020, against a 2013/2014 baseline (Marks and Spencer, 2014: 27).	
	• Ensure that electricity purchased for Marks and Spencer operated stores and offices in the UK and Republic of Ireland is from renewable sources (Marks and Spencer, 2014: 27).	In 2013/2014, all of the electricity purchased for Marks and Spencer's stores, offices and general merchandise warehouses in the UK and Republic of Ireland came from green tariff renewable sources (Marks and Spencer, 2014: 27).
	• Achieve a 35% improvement in fuel efficiency in UK and Republic of Ireland food deliveries to stores by 2015 against a 2006/2007 baseline (Marks and Spencer, 2014: 27).	Marks and Spencer achieved a 32% improvement in fuel efficiency in 2013/2014 compared to the 2006/2007 baseline (Marks and Spencer, 2014: 27).
	• Reduce UK and Republic of Ireland store refrigeration gas carbon emissions by 80% by 2020 against a 2006/2007 baseline (Marks and Spencer, 2014: 28).	In 2013/2014, refrigeration gas carbon emissions were 73% below the 2006/2007 baseline (Marks and Spencer, 2014: 28).
	• Require Marks and Spencer's top 100 clothing factories to install energy-efficient lighting and improved insulation and temperature controls to reduce their energy usage by an estimated 10% by 2015 (Marks and Spencer, 2014: 22).	Eighty-five of Marks and Spencer's top 100 clothing suppliers have now adopted energy efficiency best practices on lighting, insulation and temperature control (Marks and Spencer, 2014: 22).

(continued)

Table 4.3 *(continued)*

Company	Selected targets	Comments on performance
Morrisons	• Reduce total operational (electricity, gas, transport, waste, employee work travel, business miles, refrigeration) greenhouse gas emissions by 30% by 2020 against a 2005 baseline (Wm Morrison, 2013: 45).	By the end of 2012, Morrisons had reduced its operational greenhouse gas emissions by 19.3% against its 2005 baseline (Wm Morrison, 2013: 45).
Sainsbury's	• Reduce operational emissions by 30% in absolute terms and by 65% in relative terms (per unit of floor area) by 2020 compared to a 2005 baseline, as part of a broader target to reduce absolute greenhouse gas emissions by 50% by 2030 (J Sainsbury, 2011b: 9–10, 2013).	Sainsbury's reduced its operational emissions by 7.8% over the period 2010 to 2013 (J Sainsbury, 2013).
	• Work with Sainsbury's own-brand suppliers to reduce carbon emissions across all of Sainsbury's own-brand products by 50% in relative terms (J Sainsbury, 2011a, 2011b: 9–10, 2013).	Since 2007, Sainsburys has worked with 2,500 farmers in its Farmer Development Groups to achieve a total saving of 70,570 tonnes of carbon dioxide equivalent (J Sainsbury, 2013).
Tesco	• Halve emissions per square foot from Tesco's stores and distribution centres by 2020 compared to 2006 (Tesco, 2013: 39).	Tesco has reduced the emissions per unit of floor area from its stores and distribution centres by 34.7% over the period 2006/2007 to 2013/2014 (Tesco, 2014a: 35).
	• Reduce distribution emissions per case of goods delivered by 25% by 2020 from a 2011 baseline (Tesco, 2014a: 29).	Tesco has reduced its emissions per case transported by 7.8% over the period 2011/2012 to 2013/2014 (Tesco, 2014a: 29).

Company	Selected targets	Comments on performance
John Lewis Partnership (including Waitrose)	• Reduce operational greenhouse gas emissions by 15% by 2020/2021 against a 2010/2011 baseline (John Lewis Partnership, 2014: 33).	The partnership's emissions have increased by approximately 8% since the 2010/2011 baseline (John Lewis Partnership, 2014: 33), although, in 2012, it had noted that it expected emissions to increase for a short period before coming down (John Lewis Partnership, 2012: 55).
	• By 2015, reduce leakage of refrigerant to no more than 10% of entrained volume (John Lewis Partnership, 2014: 36).	
	• Reduce absolute greenhouse gas emissions from transport by 15% by 2020/2021 against a 2010/2011 baseline (John Lewis Partnership, 2014: 39).	John Lewis Partnership previously had a target of reducing energy-related greenhouse gas emissions per unit sales from transport CO_2 by 15% by year-end 2013/2014 relative to a 2005/2006 baseline. It did not meet this target, achieving a 10% reduction (John Lewis Partnership, 2014: 39).

Table 4.4 Ambition and duration of UK supermarkets' targets

Company	Target	Scope	Relative or absolute emission reduction?	Annualised rate of change (%/year)	Duration (years)
Asda	Reduce total greenhouse gas emissions (from energy use, refrigeration, transport, water and travel) by 10% by 2015 against a 2005 baseline.	Operations	Absolute	1.05	10
	Support Walmart's objective to eliminate 20 million tonnes of embedded carbon from its global supply chain by the end of 2015.	Supply chain	Not specified	Not specified	10
	Maintain flat energy use for the period 2012 to 2020.	Operations	Absolute	0	8
	Reduce emissions from transport by 60% per case delivered by 2015, against a 2005 baseline.	Operations (transport)	Relative	8.76	10
Co-operative Group	Reduce gross greenhouse gas emissions from the Co-operative Group's operations by 50% by 2020, against a 2006 baseline.	Operations	Absolute	4.84	14
Marks and Spencer	Improve energy efficiency in UK and Republic of Ireland stores by 35% per square foot by 2015 and by 50% by 2020, against a 2006/2007 baseline.	Operations (energy use)	Relative	5.24 (9 years) 4.84 (14 years)	14
	Improve energy efficiency in international stores, offices and distribution centres outside of the Republic of Ireland stores by 20% by 2020, against a 2013/2014 baseline.	Operations (energy use)	Relative	3.14	7
	Achieve a 35% improvement in fuel efficiency in UK and Republic of Ireland food deliveries to stores by 2015 against a 2006/2007 baseline.	Operations (transport)	Relative	4.67	9

Company	Target	Scope	Relative or absolute emission reduction?	Annualised rate of change (%/year)	Duration (years)
Morrisons	Reduce total operational (electricity, gas, transport, waste, employee work travel, business miles, refrigeration) greenhouse gas emissions by 30% by 2020 against a 2005 baseline.	Operations (electricity, gas, transport, waste, employee work travel, business miles, refrigeration)	Absolute	2.35	15
Sainsbury's	Reduce operational greenhouse gas emissions by 30% in absolute terms by 2020 compared to a 2005 baseline.	Operations	Absolute	2.35	15
	Reduce operational greenhouse gas emissions per unit of floor area by 65% by 2020 compared to a 2005 baseline.	Operations (energy use)	Relative	6.76	15
	Reduce operational greenhouse gas emissions by 50% by 2030 compared to a 2005 baseline.	Operations	Absolute	2.73	25
Tesco	To be a zero-carbon business by 2050 without purchasing offsets.	Operations (including business travel)	Absolute	See Note 1	See Note 1
	Cut supply chain emissions by 30% by 2020 against a 2008 baseline.	Supply chain	Absolute	2.93	12

(continued)

Table 4.4 (continued)

Company	Target	Scope	Relative or absolute emission reduction?	Annualised rate of change (%/year)	Duration (years)
	Identify ways to help Tesco's customers halve their carbon footprints by 2020 against a 2009 baseline.	Customers	Not specified	6.11	11
	Halve emissions per square foot from Tesco's stores and distribution centres by 2020 compared to 2006.	Operations (existing stores)	Relative	4.83	14
	Reduce distribution emissions per case of goods delivered by 25% by 2020 from a 2011 baseline.	Operations (transport)	Relative	3.15	9
John Lewis Partnership (including Waitrose)	Reduce operational greenhouse gas emissions by 15% by 2020/2021 against a 2010/2011 baseline.	Operations	Absolute	1.61	10
	Reduce absolute greenhouse gas emissions from transport by 15% by 2020/2021 against a 2010/2011 baseline.	Operations (transport)	Absolute	1.61	10

1 Tesco's target relies heavily on the generation or purchase of renewable energy to deliver this target, and so it is not possible to calculate an annual percentage improvement in energy efficiency.

5 Governance and corporate action on climate change

International experiences

In Chapter 4 we examined how external governance pressures and international governance conditions had affected the climate change strategies and responses of firms within the UK supermarket sector. From this analysis, we can draw six high-level conclusions:

- Weak external pressures can, if they are aligned, have a significant influence on internal governance processes and on corporate strategies and actions.
- Internal governance processes strongly influence the responsiveness of organisations to external pressures and the degree to which companies institutionalise their responses to these pressures within their businesses.
- External governance pressures, internal governance conditions and corporate responses not only co-exist but also interact dynamically with each other.
- Companies will generally only invest capital in situations when there is a clear financial case for action (i.e. where the benefits outweigh the costs, when the rate of return meets or exceeds company targets).
- The willingness of stakeholders to get involved in the governance of corporations depends on whether the issue in question (in this case climate change) is a priority for them, whether they have the capacity to get involved, whether they have the expertise to get involved, and whether the right accountability processes and tools are available to them.
- Companies' responses – their management systems and processes, the actions they take, their communications – enable them to deflect certain external pressures and to weaken others.

The question we consider in this chapter is whether these findings are unique to the UK or whether they have more general applicability. We explore this by analysing the climate change strategies of the world's 25 largest retailers as listed in Table 5.1 (excluding Tesco, which we covered in the UK case-study), and the internal and external factors that have shaped these strategies. We group these retailers by country of origin or country of listing. This provides us with five distinct business contexts to examine, namely the United States (US), Japan, France, Germany and Australia.

Table 5.1 The top 25 global retailers in 2012

Rank	Company	Country of origin
1	Walmart Stores	United States
2	Tesco	UK
3	Costco Wholesale	United States
4	Carrefour	France
5	The Kroger Co.	United States
6	Schwarz Unternehmens Treuhand (Lidl)	Germany
7	Metro	Germany
8	Home Depot	United States
9	Aldi Einkauf GmbH & Co.	Germany
10	Target	United States
11	Walgreen Company (Walgreens)	United States
12	CVS Caremark	United States
13	Aeon	Japan
14	Groupe Auchan	France
15	Woolworths	Australia
16	Amazon.com	United States
17	Seven & i Holdings	Japan
18	Edeka Zentrale	Germany
19	Wesfarmers	Australia
20	Casino Guichard-Perrachon	France
21	Lowe's Companies	United States
22	REWE Group	Germany
23	Best Buy Company	United States
24	Centres Distributeurs E. Leclerc	France
25	Safeway Inc.	United States

(Deloitte, 2014: G12–G13)

Across the five countries and over the period 2000 to 2015, we see many common features. All of the retailers faced severe cost and competitive pressures. All of the retailers faced some pressure, notably in the period 2005 to 2007, to take action to reduce their greenhouse gas emissions. All of the retailers established energy and climate change management systems and processes, and all took action to reduce their operational emissions.

We also see some striking differences. The external governance pressures that the retailers faced and the specific stakeholders involved in exerting these pressures differed between countries and even between companies within a particular country. The companies reached different conclusions about the business importance of corporate responsibility issues in general and climate change in particular. The actions taken by companies to reduce their emissions and the attention paid to customer and supply chain-related emissions differed.

Together, these commonalities and differences allow us to refine our analysis, both to draw more generally applicable conclusions about the relationship between external governance processes, internal governance conditions and corporate strategies, and to identify the specific characteristics of external governance pressures, internal governance conditions and corporate responses that are of particular importance in determining the outcomes that are achieved.

The United States

The US is estimated to be the world's second (after China) largest grocery market (IGD, 2013). The 11 US retailers included in Deloitte's 2014 list of the world's 25 largest retailers were Amazon, Best Buy, Costco, CVS Caremark, Home Depot, Kroger, Lowe's Companies, Safeway, Target, Walgreens and Walmart (Deloitte, 2014).

Governance from the outside: weak drivers for change

The starting point for our discussion of US retailers' approach to climate change is that, in the period 2000 to 2015, the pressures for US corporations to take action on climate change were significantly weaker than in the UK. Energy and electricity prices in the US were significantly lower, typically one-half to two-thirds of those in the UK (see, generally, DECC (2014: 59, 62, 65, 68)). Furthermore, the US government, notwithstanding the 2014 US–China climate change agreement (where the US committed to reducing its greenhouse gas emissions by 26–28% below its 2005 levels by 2025 [US White House, Office of the Press Secretary, 2014]), was seen as a laggard on climate change. The US had been reluctant to contribute to strong international action on climate change and was unwilling to introduce domestic measures that would penalise US businesses (IEEP and NRDC, 2008; Kelemen and Vogel, 2010; ICF, 2012; RobecoSAM, 2013; Sullivan and Gouldson, 2016).

Climate change did attract more business attention in the period 2005–2007. As in the UK, the Stern Review on the Economics of Climate Change and Al Gore's film *An Inconvenient Truth* received significant media coverage, and there was an increased business awareness of energy costs. Around this time, many of the US retailers – in their own corporate responsibility reports or in their responses to the CDP– started to highlight the potential for emissions trading or other economic instruments to increase energy prices. Most, however, qualified these observations by stating that they considered the introduction of such legislation to be relatively unlikely and that, even if the Federal government did take substantive action on climate change, it was unlikely to allow energy prices to rise significantly.

While the regulatory and policy drivers for action were consistently weak, a number of retailers did identify the potential for consumer interest in climate change to increase over time. These retailers explained that they expected their climate change strategies to enable them to pre-empt and proactively respond to consumer questions and demands. Mirroring the findings from the UK, the retailers reported that they had seen limited evidence that companies' performance on climate change was an important influence on where consumers chose to shop. A number did note that they had seen tangible consumer demand in relation to electrical and electronic products.

Internal governance processes: climate change as an operational issue

Compared to the UK supermarkets, sustainability reporting by the US retailers lagged by almost a decade. The first sustainability or equivalent reports from the major US retailers were produced by Lowe's (in 2004) and Target (in 2005), with reporting on climate change-related issues lagging reporting on energy or sustainability-related issues by a number of years. Perhaps the most extreme example of this lag is Lowe's, which issued its first corporate responsibility report in 2004 but only published its first greenhouse gas emissions inventory in 2012 (Lowe's, 2012). Other examples include Kroger, which produced its first sustainability report in 2007 (Kroger, 2007) and its first greenhouse gas emissions inventory in 2009 (Kroger, 2009: 8), and Costco, which produced its first sustainability report in 2009 (Costco, 2009) and its first greenhouse gas emissions inventory in 2011 (Costco, 2011: 13–14).

The weaknesses in the external pressures for action on climate change were reflected in the manner in which US retailers managed their greenhouse gas emissions. Even by 2015, the majority were not providing particularly well-developed accounts of the relationships between climate change, energy and sustainability-related issues and wider business strategy. The primary narrative on energy and climate change related to short-term financial returns, with limited discussion of longer-term factors (e.g. business resilience) or of brand and intangibles when discussing these issues. This was illustrated by a 2013 report from the (US) Retail Industry Leaders Association (RILA), which stated that most retailers expected their energy-related investments to provide a two- to three-year payback (RILA, 2013: 16–17; similar findings were reported in CDP [2013b: 47]). RILA did qualify this finding somewhat by commenting that top-performing companies may look for paybacks 'as far out as three to five years' (RILA, 2013: 17, 18).

There are differences between the targets set by US retailers and those set by UK supermarkets. As discussed in Chapter 4, by 2015 most of the UK super-markets had set long-term, absolute emission reduction targets for their operations, and a number had also set targets for their supply chain and value chain-related emissions. In contrast, as indicated in Table 5.2, US retailers continued to focus more narrowly on operational and transport-related emissions; most of the targets focused on relative emissions and were set over relatively short timeframes.

It is however important to acknowledge that while the US retailers had not set targets that were as ambitious as those of their UK counterparts, the US retailers had committed substantial sums to energy efficiency and renewable energy. Examples include Walmart's 2005 commitment to investing approximately $500 million annually in technologies that increase energy and fuel efficiency in the US (Walmart, 2009a: 21), Target's investment of over $120 million in energy efficiency retrofits and renewable energy projects between 2008 and the end of 2011 (Target, 2012) and Home Depot's investment of over $250 million in systems and energy-efficient upgrades for its stores in the period 2004 to 2010 (Home Depot, 2012).

Corporate strategies and responses: focus on efficiency

Improving energy efficiency in buildings and transport was a long-running (dating back to at least the mid-1990s) objective for US retailers. The actions taken were broadly similar to those taken by the UK retailers – upgrading of control, lighting, refrigeration and HVAC systems, installing doors on coolers and freezers, adopting energy management systems, purchasing more efficient vehicles, improving logistics, and providing employee training and education (see, for example, RILA, 2012, 2013). Renewable energy was a particular focus. In fact, many retailers were included on the USEPA's list of the top 20 on-site generators of renewable energy (RILA, 2012: 16).

When we look at those retailers where at least three years' worth of data are available (see Table 5.3), we see that five succeeded in reducing their absolute greenhouse gas emissions whereas three saw their greenhouse gas emissions increase. Overall, acknowledging the relatively short time periods involved, the rate of improvement achieved by the US retailers lagged that of the UK supermarkets by approximately 0.5% per annum; US retailers averaged a 0.6% per annum reduction in their greenhouse gas emissions whereas the UK retailers achieved almost twice that, averaging a 1.1% per annum reduction. A similar finding emerges when we look at emissions intensity. UK supermarkets reduced their energy and/or emissions intensity by approximately 4% per annum over periods of five or seven years. In contrast, the two US retailers (CVS Caremark and Walmart) that provided sufficient data to allow these calculations reduced their energy and/or emissions intensity by slightly less than 3% per annum over a five or six-year period (CVS Caremark 2012: 53, 2013: 45, 2014: 37; Walmart, 2014); again, this is approximately half the rate of improvement achieved by the UK retailers. Because of data gaps, it is difficult to make a complete assessment of the likely trajectory of absolute greenhouse emissions from the US retailers. However, Table 5.3, which is based on five companies' comments on how they expected their emissions to evolve over time, suggests that US retailers saw a clear tension between business growth and emission reductions.

While reducing supply chain emissions was a priority for UK supermarkets, US retailers paid relatively little attention to their supply chains in the years

2000 to 2015 (see, generally, RILA, 2013: 31). When they did engage with suppliers, the focus was on those aspects that directly affected the retailer (e.g. product packaging, which has direct implications for transport costs), rather than on aspects such as production processes or supplier energy management. There were some signs of change towards the end of the period covered by our research. In 2013, RILA suggested that the use of life-cycle assessment would grow significantly and that some of the retailers had encouraged their purchasing teams to integrate sustainability-related factors (e.g. energy use) into their supplier selection and related processes (RILA, 2013: 32, 38–39). At around the same time, a few US retailers started to talk about the environmental characteristics of their supply chains. For example, in its 2012 sustainability report, Kroger presented case-studies of how two of its farm suppliers had reduced their carbon footprint (Kroger, 2012b: 15, 16), although it was not clear what contribution Kroger had actually made to these outcomes.

Walmart was the major exception to this discussion on US retailers' supply chain practices. Walmart identified its supply chain as an important area of focus, and set a target of eliminating 20 million tonnes of greenhouse gas emissions from the life-cycle of the products it sells by 2015 (Walmart, 2014: 101). Walmart took various actions to meet this goal including measuring energy use and emissions throughout its supply chain, hosting supplier conferences, setting goals (e.g. to improve energy efficiency by 20% per unit of production by 2012 against a 2007 baseline in the top 200 factories in China from which it sourced directly), and assessing supplier performance on energy, climate change, natural resources, and material efficiency (Walmart, 2014: 101–106). In 2014, Walmart reported that it had eliminated 7.575 million tonnes of greenhouse gas emissions by the end of 2013 and had implemented projects that it estimated would eliminate 18 million tonnes of greenhouse gas emissions by the end of 2015 (Walmart, 2014: 101).

As noted above, the US retailers were of the view that US consumers had relatively limited interest in climate change, although a notable exception related to electrical products. From 2009 or 2010, many of the US retailers started to offer energy-efficient products (e.g. consumer electronics) and energy-saving products (with low-energy light bulbs being particularly popular). These retailers also highlighted their participation in programmes such as the USEPA's Energy Star programme, and proactively advertised the financial savings associated with the use of more efficient products. For example, Best Buy argued that its focus on energy-efficient technologies and purchasing renewable energy would lead to better customer loyalty, given that its consumers were increasingly seeking environmentally preferable products (Best Buy, 2013). Interesting, some retailers went further than individual products and started to offer wider product ranges. One example was Home Depot's Eco Options Program, which offered a range of climate-friendly consumer products such as energy-efficient windows and doors, insulation, caulking and sealing products, smart home technology and LED lights.

The interactions between external governance pressures, internal governance conditions and corporate responses

There are many parallels in the journeys taken by UK supermarkets and US retailers. Both started by focusing on energy efficiency (which is generally where the most immediate financial opportunities can be found). They both – albeit with a significant lag in the case of the US – subsequently focused on greenhouse gas emissions as well as energy use, started to set longer-term targets and – in the case of UK retailers – broadened the scope of action from their own operations to a wider focus on the supply and value chain. Despite the many commonalities, by 2015 it was clear that UK supermarkets had succeeded in reducing their greenhouse gas emissions more quickly than their US counterparts, that UK supermarkets were setting more ambitious targets and that UK supermarkets were paying much greater attention to their wider environmental footprints.

The primary conclusion to be drawn from this is that the weaker external governance pressures that characterised the US from 2000 onwards resulted in US retailers having weaker internal governance processes and weaker corporate responses on climate change. Lower energy prices meant that reducing energy costs was a lower priority for US retailers, and that relatively fewer projects would meet the target rates of return on investment required by US retailers. Furthermore, the fact that US retailers framed climate change as primarily being an issue of cost savings and business efficiency meant that they did not see climate change as an issue that had wider strategic implications for their businesses. Even though the period 2005 to 2007 was a key tipping point for UK retailers, the fact that the US government did not or was unable to take strong regulatory action at this point was interpreted by US retailers as confirmation that strong regulatory action was unlikely, and that they could continue to treat climate change as an issue of operational rather than strategic importance.

The other important conclusion from the US case-study is that the wider business context, and not just the specific details of climate change and energy-related debates, is important. This is illustrated by the role played by sector peer pressure in the US and the UK. In stark contrast to the UK supermarket sector, peer pressure was relatively unimportant in the US retail sector. For example, none of the other retailers sought to match or better Walmart's supply chain-related commitments. On climate change, as with other sustainability issues, US retailers tended to be tentative and to wait to see what benefits or outcomes accrued to leadership companies, before looking to follow.

The importance of context is also illustrated by the different approaches adopted to supply chain-related emissions. The relationship between US retailers and their suppliers is qualitatively different to that between the UK supermarkets and their suppliers. UK supermarkets have close and long-term relationships with, and significant influence over, many of their suppliers, in particular for own-brand and agricultural products. In contrast, US retailers tend to have relatively little influence on their supply chains, and relatively little direct engagement with them (on issues such as environmental management). This is compounded by the fact that most of the US retailers had relatively small sustainability teams, limiting their ability to work closely with the companies in their supply chains.

Japan

This section focuses on Aeon and Seven & i Holdings, the two Japanese retailers in the world's 25 largest retailers. In 2012, based on turnover, these two companies were both over three times larger than the third largest retailer in Japan (Deloitte, 2014: G12).

Governance from the outside: public policy and corporate conformance

In Japan, the primary drivers for corporate action on climate change have come from the Japanese government. Japan played a leading role in international negotiations around climate change and biodiversity at the Rio Summit in 1992 and in the subsequent Kyoto Protocol in 1997. This leadership played an important role in stimulating Japanese corporate action on environmental and climate change issues. In the mid to late 1990s, many large Japanese companies established formal environmental management systems and started to report on their social and environmental performance.

These international efforts were supported by legislation and by a variety of domestic policy announcements and commitments. The ratification of the Kyoto Protocol in 2005 was followed by, among others, the introduction of the Japanese Energy Saving Law and the Global Warming Law in 2006, and the Tokyo Climate Change Strategy in 2007. In July 2008, Japan announced a national greenhouse gas emission reduction target of 50% by 2050 against a 2008 baseline, and in 2009 a further target of reducing emissions by 15% below 2005 levels by 2020 (CDP, 2009: 20). In March 2010, Japan established emission reduction targets of 25% by 2020 and 80% by 2050 (against a 1990 baseline in both cases), and committed to 10% of Japan's primary energy supply being generated by renewable energy by 2020 (CDP, 2010: 17).

In the Japanese business community, it is hugely important to be seen to be 'doing the right thing'. When the Japanese government takes action on an issue, even if the action is not directly targeted at companies, Japanese companies feel that it is important that they demonstrate their commitment to action. This phenomenon has been seen in relation to climate change. The above domestic policy interventions catalysed corporate action on climate change. A number of industry sectors adopted voluntary action plans, and companies – including retailers – participated in a Japanese Ministry of Economy, Trade and Industry voluntary local emissions trading scheme (see, for example, Japan Chain Stores Association 2014; Japan Franchise Chain Association, 2014; Keidanren, 2013).

The 2011 Fukushima nuclear crisis and shutdown following the Great East Earthquake significantly changed the climate change policy debate in Japan.

Restrictions on power consumption were imposed in 2011 and 2012. These included scheduled blackouts in some areas and, during the summer months, the National Power-Saving Edict required large energy users (i.e. those whose contract demand was more than 500kW) to reduce electricity consumption by 15% from the previous year during weekday hours (CDP, 2011: 20). The disaster also forced the Japanese government to consider a complete overhaul of its basic energy plan, not least because Japan's medium and long-term greenhouse gas emission reduction targets were based on the assumption that nuclear power would provide 80% of Japan's electricity needs (CDP, 2011: 20).

Internal governance processes: focus on costs

Japanese companies have been in the vanguard of environmental and corporate responsibility reporting, and Aeon and Seven & i are no exceptions. Aeon published its first environmental report in 1996. This report provided data on its store and office-related greenhouse gas emissions and energy use, and Aeon has continued to provide these data annually since that time, adding data on transport-related emissions since 2008. Seven & i was established in September 2005; it first responded to the CDP in 2006 and produced its first corporate responsibility report in 2007. In 2009, Seven & i conducted a third-party review of the greenhouse gas emissions data for its major operating companies, and in 2010, it produced a company-wide manual to encourage better and more standardised calculation processes (Seven & i Holdings, 2009a: 24–25, 2010: 14).

Both companies established structured environmental or corporate responsibility management systems and processes. In 2000, the entire Aeon organisation was certified to the ISO14001 standard (Aeon, 2001: 2). Seven & i established a formal environmental governance and oversight structure when it was first formed. This included a corporate responsibility department responsible for managing operational issues and policy implementation, a board committee with oversight of its environmental performance, and an environmental committee consisting of a representative from each of its major operating companies' boards (Seven & I Holdings, 2011: 56, 2012a: 8).

Aeon's corporate targets evolved in a similar manner to the UK retailers, moving from relatively short-term, efficiency-focused targets to longer-term absolute emission reduction targets. From 1998 to 2007, its targets were broadly to stabilise or modestly reduce greenhouse gas emissions and energy consumption on a year-by-year basis. In 2008, Aeon announced its Global Warming Manifesto, committing itself to reducing its greenhouse gas emissions by 30% by 2012 against a 2006 baseline, to be achieved through reducing emissions from stores, from product and distribution, through working with customers and through offsetting (Aeon, 2008a: 5). Aeon achieved this goal in 2011, a year ahead of schedule (Aeon, 2012a: 27). In 2011, Aeon formulated a new sustainability strategy which included targets to reduce its Japanese greenhouse gas emissions (the major part of the group) by 20% by 2013 against a

2006 baseline (Aeon, 2011: 12–14), to develop eco-stores that achieved a 50% reduction in greenhouse gas emissions compared to conventional stores, and to reduce fuel use by 10% over the period 2010 to 2013 (Aeon, 2011: 13–14). Aeon also committed to increase the number of products with carbon labels from 21 to 100 over 2010 to 2013 (Aeon, 2011: 13–14). Aeon subsequently reported on its progress against these objectives, although with a clear shift in emphasis from absolute to relative performance measures; in its 2012 report, it reported on both total emissions and on emissions per unit area, whereas it only reported on emissions per unit area in its 2013 report (Aeon, 2012a: 23–24, 2013: 23–24).

While Seven & i also set targets, it consistently stated that it saw the expansion and development of new stores and new products as inevitable, even though this expansion would lead to increases in electricity consumption and greenhouse gas emissions (Seven & i Holdings, 2007b, 2012a: 7). For example, in 2007 it stated that rather than setting an emission reduction target or limiting the total store area, it would improve its environmental efficiency through the installation of the latest energy-efficient facilities and through improved management practices (Seven & i Holdings, 2007b). In its 2012 CDP response, Seven & i stated that it had established targets for Seven-Eleven Japan stores (to reduce electricity consumption per unit of floor area per hour by 1% per annum) and for its Ito-Yokado stores (to reduce the greenhouse gas emissions from its operations on a per unit of floor area per hour basis by 1% per annum) (Seven & i Holdings, 2012b). Despite these commitments, it did not set an overarching greenhouse gas emission reduction target.

It is also relevant to note that, acknowledging the targets that have been set, both companies were clear that the actions taken and the investments made needed to provide commercial returns. Aeon and Seven & i applied similar criteria to their energy efficiency and emission reductions investments, expecting these to provide payback periods of between three and four years (Aeon, 2012b; Seven & i Holdings, 2009b). Both also consistently identified energy costs and potential increases in energy costs as a key driver for action, noting that these costs may increase as a result of carbon taxes and other measures that affect energy prices and/or impose costs on greenhouse gas emissions (see, for example, Aeon, 2008b, 2012b).

Corporate strategies and responses: efficiency, offsets and labelling

Both companies had a long track record of taking action to reduce the greenhouse gas emissions from their operations. Among other measures, they improved the efficiency of air-conditioning and refrigeration equipment, increased the use of low-energy lighting, improved their monitoring and control systems, reduced refrigerant gas emissions, installed night covers on open-top display freezers and installed solar panels in some stores (Aeon, 2001: 36, 2002: 39, 46, 2005: 11, 2008a: 15, 2013: 27–28; Seven & i Holdings, 2009a: 25–31, 2012a: 20–22, 38, 43). They accelerated their efforts to improve energy efficiency following the Fukushima disaster. For example, Seven-Eleven Japan – part of Seven & i – replaced existing lighting with LED lights inside stores, installed solar panels, and took other measures with the aim of reducing its electricity consumption by about 20% compared to the previous year (Seven & i Holdings, 2011: 4).

Reducing greenhouse gas emissions from vehicle fleets by improving vehicle efficiency, optimising logistics and driver training were also priority areas for action (Aeon, 2005: 11, 2008a: 15, 2013: 31; Seven & i Holdings, 2009a: 17, 29, 2012a: 20–26). In a similar manner to the UK supermarkets, Aeon and Seven & i used their target-setting processes to ensure that technology and other innovations are shared across their businesses. They developed 'eco-stores' which consumed 20–30% less energy than conventional stores, committed to rolling out new energy-efficient technologies and approaches across their businesses, and established structured processes for sharing knowledge and expertise across their businesses (Aeon, 2008a: 15, 2013: 29; Seven & i Holdings, 2010: 4, 2012a: 22, 2012b).

When we look at Aeon's store and office-related greenhouse gas emissions and energy consumption, we see that it reduced its total greenhouse gas emissions by approximately 6% over the period 2000 to 2012. Increases in electricity (by approximately 14% over this period) and gas (approximately 11%) consumption, were offset by reductions in greenhouse gas emissions from refrigeration (Aeon, 2001: 4–5, 2002: 5, 2003: 43, 2004: 38, 2005: 39, 2006: 42, 2007: 41, 2008a: 19, 2009b: 3, 2010: 19, 2011: 22, 2012a: 70, 2013: 78). While the data for Seven & i are more limited, its 2013 corporate responsibility report indicated that total greenhouse gas emissions from its store operations had increased by approximately 15% over the period 2010 to 2012 (Seven & i Holdings, 2013: 43). Seven & i commented that business growth, introduction of new services, increase in the number of stores, introduction of new stores with larger floor areas and longer operating hours had all led to increases in energy demand and, hence, emissions (Seven & i Holdings, 2007a: 55, 2008: 31, 2009a: 26, 2010: 26, 2012b).

Offsetting was a major element of both companies' approaches. In 2009, Seven & i launched a tropical forest conservation programme, and donated money to the International Tropical Timber Organization (ITTO) to conserve 58,000 hectares in Indonesia. Seven and i estimated that this programme reduced carbon dioxide emissions by 1.2 million tonnes in its first year, equivalent to over half of the emissions from its major domestic (i.e. Japanese) operating companies (Seven & i Holdings, 2008: 21, 2009a: 24, 2010: 4, 18, 2012a: 20–21). Aeon had a long-running (over 20 years) tree planting programme, both within Japan and internationally (Aeon, 2001: 2, 2006: 10, 2009a: 13–14).

Finally, both companies took action to reduce their supply chain and value chain-related emissions; they participated in the Japanese Ministry of Economy, Trade and Industry's Greenhouse Gases Footprint Working Group, and made commitments on product labelling. Seven & i stated that it would strive to reduce greenhouse gas emissions across its entire supply chain; it calculated carbon footprints for a number of food products and household goods, and stated that it intended working with its business partners to reduce these emissions (Seven & i Holdings, 2008: 21, 2011: 17). Aeon sold products with the Japanese government's carbon footprint label (Aeon, 2010: 10) and made commitments to increase the number of products with such labels. Both also offered products that would reduce customer energy use (e.g. functional underwear which allowed customers to lower their household temperatures, LEDs) and encouraged customers to purchase carbon offsets to offset the carbon footprint of their shopping (Aeon, 2008a: 11, 2010: 15, 23, 2011: 26–28, 2012a: 31; Seven & i Holdings, 2012a: 20, 35).

Wider reflections on governance processes in Japan

In both the UK and Japan, the actions taken by the large retailers delivered consistent and sustained improvements in energy efficiency improvements in buildings and in transport. However, when we move beyond buildings and transport, a different picture emerges. By 2015, the UK retailers had set long-term (to 2030 and beyond) absolute emission reduction targets, whereas the two Japanese retailers were continuing to set shorter-term targets directed at improving their relative (i.e. per unit of turnover) rather than absolute performance. The UK retailers were explicitly talking about the efforts they were making to reduce greenhouse gas emissions in their supply chains but the Japanese retailers were providing limited information about their work with suppliers. Finally, the Japanese retailers were emphasising tree planting and emissions offsetting as integral parts of their carbon reduction strategies, but the UK retailers were saying relatively little about these sorts of activities.

These differences reflect differences in the external governance pressures faced by UK and Japanese companies, and differences in the business environment within these countries. From our research, three differences are of particular importance. First, while corporate reputation is hugely important to retailers in both countries, its manifestations are quite different. As noted above, being seen to be doing the right thing is hugely important in Japan. This starts with regulatory compliance, and then tends to emphasise symbolic and philanthropic actions that enable companies to demonstrate their commitment to action. Examples from the Japanese retailers include their tree planting and offset programmes (which allow them to demonstrate their commitment to their consumers) and their participation in voluntary initiatives (which allow them to demonstrate their commitment to government). In contrast, the UK retailers see that their corporate reputation depends on the actions that they take within their business or in their supply chains, and the manner in which they engage with their stakeholders.

The second is that peer pressure manifests itself in quite different ways between the two countries (Kuroda et al., 2014). UK supermarkets compete with each other on the basis of their approach to corporate responsibility, with a strong emphasis on leadership. In contrast, Japanese retailers seem to cluster, with relatively little active differentiation on the basis of their corporate responsibility efforts. In practice, this means that if one Japanese retailer adopts a new innovation, its industry peers tend to copy that innovation but do not go further. This is compounded by the fact that the Japanese retail market – in terms of its approach to corporate responsibility – tends to be relatively insular. It is interesting that those Japanese companies with a more international focus (e.g. Fast Retailing – the owner of Uniqlo – which has a significant presence in Europe) have, over time, tended to have a similar focus to the UK supermarkets in terms of the subjects they cover in their corporate responsibility reports and other communications.

The third is that consumer and NGO pressures are very different. UK consumers are very concerned about climate change and the UK has an active and effective NGO community. In contrast, climate change does not appear to be a major issue for Japanese consumers, with consumers' expectations of companies being correspondingly low. Interestingly, Aeon and Seven & i, while acknowledging the weaknesses in consumer pressure, both identified the importance of ensuring that they were prepared for a strengthening of consumer pressures. For example, Seven & i stated that it was managing consumer-related risks through its efforts to reduce emissions and energy, through offering green/environmentally friendly products and through proactively communicating its efforts (e.g. in its corporate responsibility report, through its website) (Seven & i Holdings, 2009b, 2012b). Moreover, Japanese NGOs have tended to be relatively weak and lack the influence and capacity to hold companies to account. This may be changing thanks to the activities of the Japanese branches of international NGOs such as Friends of the Earth and Greenpeace, and the emergence of more effective domestic NGOs such as the Japan Renewable Energy Foundation.

Finally, the Fukushima disaster offers some interesting insights into the implications of shocks to systems. In the case of Japan, the general picture was that through the 2000s companies continued to improve their energy efficiency but saw greenhouse gas emissions grow in the period leading up to the Great East Earthquake. The Great East Earthquake placed huge pressure on the electricity grid and led to companies making step-change (between 10 and 20%) reductions in their electricity consumption through a combination of changing practices (e.g. switching off equipment) and investments in more efficient equipment (e.g. LEDs). These measures were driven both by regulatory pressure and the desire to be seen to be doing the right thing and respond to societal expectations. However, the reductions in energy consumption were temporary and companies' energy use subsequently rose again, with their emissions rising more quickly because of the greater proportion of fossil fuels in the generating mix. While we should be careful about drawing strong conclusions, this does suggest that the effect of one-off shocks, even if dramatic, are likely to be quite different to external governance pressures or drivers that are sustained over longer periods (or seen as more permanent changes to the business landscape). From an internal governance perspective, it suggests that unless companies already see climate change as a long-term strategic value driver, one-off events (unless they are repeated) are unlikely to make a significant change to management's views.

Germany

The major German retailers (in terms of their percentage of market share in Germany in 2012) are Edeka (20.5%), Schwarz/Lidl (15.1%), Aldi (13.6%), REWE Group (12.2%) and Metro (4.3%) (USDA, 2013). These are all ranked among the 25 largest global retailers (Deloitte, 2014).

Discounting external governance pressures

German consumers are highly price sensitive. This has led to the German supermarket sector being dominated by discount retailers (Bleher, 2013; USDA, 2013). With price being the primary point of competition and differentiation in the sector, the primary motivation for the German retailers to act on climate change is cost. For example, REWE Group stated that the costs of cooling, lighting and heating stores and of transport influence how competitive a retail company is and, therefore, that conserving energy, lowering costs and reducing greenhouse gases are the main focus of its commitment to protecting the environment (REWE Group, 2009: 14, 2011: 45). Similarly, Metro identified higher energy prices and the introduction of carbon taxes as important drivers for its efforts on energy efficiency (Metro Group, 2009: 8, 2011b, 2012b).

As in the UK, the period 2005–2007 saw climate change receive much greater public and media attention, again catalysed by the Stern Review on the Economics of Climate Change (Stern, 2006), Al Gore's film *An Inconvenient Truth* and the introduction of the EU Emissions Trading Scheme in 2005. While this period saw an increase in German consumers' awareness of climate change, price continued to dominate consumers' decisions and there was limited evidence that companies' performance on climate change was an important influence on where consumers chose to shop (Bleher, 2013). This was confirmed by a REWE Group stakeholder survey from 2010, which revealed that stakeholders expected the company to provide products at affordable prices and, in addition to quality, to take responsibility for the sustainability of these products (REWE Group, 2011: 45). Notwithstanding this emphasis on price, there was evidence that German consumers did see the sustainability (or green) characteristics of individual products as important and that they were willing to pay a premium for 'sustainable' products (USDA, 2013).

Internal governance processes and cost reduction

This emphasis on price had direct consequences for the German supermarket sector's approach to sustainability. German retailers were notorious for their lack of transparency, including on sustainability-related issues, although this was justified by the sector on the grounds that such disclosures were not important sources of market advantage. With the exception of Metro, which produced its first sustainability report in 2002, the other German retailers significantly lagged their UK counterparts in terms of their sustainability or climate change reporting. REWE Group only published its first sustainability report in 2008 and its first carbon footprint in 2009, while Aldi, Lidl and Edeka, despite starting to provide some qualitative information on their websites in 2012 and 2013, had not produced comprehensive reports on their social or environmental performance by 2015. The consequence is that there is actually relatively little information available on the evolution of the German retail sector's approach to climate change in the period 2000 to 2015.

The emphasis on cost competitiveness was reflected in the investment rates of return being sought; Metro (the only German retailer for whom such information is available) reported that its investments to improve energy efficiency typically offered payback periods of one to three years (Metro, 2011b, 2012b).

Both Metro and REWE Group published information on their greenhouse gas emission reduction targets. Up to 2006, Metro's targets were a mix of process and relatively short-term performance targets. In 2006, it set a group intensity target of reducing its greenhouse gas emissions per square metre of selling space by 15% by 2015 against a 2006 baseline, although it acknowledged that it expected its absolute Scope 1 and 2 emissions to increase by 18% over this period because of its business expansion (Metro Group, 2008: 53, 2011b, 2012a: 21, 2012b). It also stated that it expected its Scope 3 emissions to increase by 25% because of expansions in its procurement logistics and its moves towards collecting goods directly from suppliers (Metro Group, 2012b). In 2013, Metro announced a new goal of reducing its greenhouse gas emissions per square metre of selling by 20% by 2020 compared to a 2011 baseline (Metro Group, 2013a: 30, 31). The target included emissions from the consumption of electricity and thermal energy, paper use, refrigerant losses from refrigeration and air-conditioning, fuel consumption in company cars and emergency power generators, and business travel (Metro Group, 2013b: 57–58, 62–64). In total, these sources accounted for almost 40% of Metro's carbon footprint (Metro Group, 2013a: 57–58). The scope and definition of this commitment differed from Metro's previous commitment, which had included emission sources such as logistics. Metro justified this change by noting that emissions from logistics were increasing at a disproportionate rate due to its expansion into countries such as China and Russia (where considerably longer transport routes are the norm) (Metro Group, 2013a: 57–58).

In 2009, REWE Group set a target of reducing its greenhouse gas emissions per square metre of sales floor space by 30% by 2015, against a 2006 baseline (REWE Group, 2009: 5; 2011: 45, 98–99). It met this target in 2012 and subsequently adopted a new target of halving its greenhouse gas emissions per unit of retail floor area by 2022 against a baseline of 2006 (REWE Group, 2014a).

Corporate responses: reducing costs

Improving energy efficiency in buildings and in transport has been a long-running (dating back to at least the mid-1990s) area of focus for all of the German retailers. Among other actions, they upgraded lighting, refrigeration and HVAC systems, installed doors on coolers and freezers, set efficiency standards for new buildings, improved the efficiency of electrical equipment, and implemented energy management systems, control technologies and monitoring and maintenance processes (see, for example, Aldi, 2011a, 2014b; Edeka, 2014a; Lidl, 2014; Metro Group, 2004: 48, 2011a: 6, 2012a: 16–17, 45–46, 2013a: 33; REWE Group, 2009: 15, 2011: 93–94, 98, 2014c). They reduced greenhouse gas emissions from refrigeration through improved monitoring and maintenance processes, and through the testing and adoption of climate-friendly refrigerants (Aldi, 2014b, 2014d; Metro Group, 2008: 46–47, 2011a: 7, 2013a: 32; REWE Group, 2009: 15, 20, 2014b). In 2013, Metro committed to only using natural refrigerants such as carbon dioxide in all of its stores by 2015 (Metro Group, 2013a: 32). In relation to transport, the retailers purchased more efficient vehicles, improved logistics, explored alternative transport options such as shipping and rail, and trained their drivers on fuel-saving measures (see, for example, Aldi, 2011a, 2014a; Edeka, 2014a, 2014b; Metro AG, 2002: 6, 8; Metro Group, 2004: 33–34, 2006: 22, 2008: 45–46, 2009: 8–9, 2012a: 38, 45–46; REWE Group, 2011: 18–19, 2014d).

Renewable energy was a particular area of focus because of its potential to significantly reduce energy costs. Each of the retailers installed geothermal and/or solar energy at a number of their facilities (Aldi, 2011a, 2014c; Edeka, 2014a; Lidl, 2014; Metro Group, 2012a: 17; REWE Group, 2011: 95, 2014c). REWE Group switched to 100% green electricity in 2008, making the REWE Group the largest user of renewable energy in Germany (REWE Group, 2009: 12–13, 16, 2011: 95, 98). REWE Group also required at least 25% of the hydroelectric power plants supplying its stores and outlets in Germany to be less than three years old, thereby providing an incentive for new renewable generation plants to be built (REWE Group, 2009: 16).

While it is not possible to make a robust assessment of how the German retailers compare to each other or to their international peers, the information provided by Metro and REWE Group does, however, allow an assessment to be made of their overall trends in performance. Metro's total Scope 1 and Scope 2 emissions (i.e. its operational emissions) increased by 18% over the period 2006 to 2011 but declined by approximately 4% from 2011 to 2013 (Metro Group, 2012b, 2013b: 3). Metro did, however, consistently improve its energy intensity (i.e. its energy consumption per square metre of selling space) by between 2 and 3% per annum over the period 2001 to 2013 (Metro Group, 2004, 2006, 2009: 8, 2011a: 6, 2012b, 2013a: 31, 2013b). REWE Group achieved similar outcomes; its total greenhouse gas emissions reduced by 6.5% (i.e. approximately 1% per annum) between 2006 and 2012, with its greenhouse gas emissions per unit of floor area declining by 31.8% or approximately 5% per annum in the same period (REWE Group, 2013: 59).

While the German retailers paid less attention to their supply chains and value chains than UK supermarkets, there were signs of change. For example, Edeka entered into a partnership with WWF, with one of the goals of the partnership being to reduce greenhouse gas emissions from some of Edeka's own-label products (Edeka, 2014a), and REWE Group participated in a product carbon footprint pilot project, along with WWF, the Öko-Institut and the Potsdam Institute for Climate Impact Research (REWE Group, 2009: 13).

In relation to customers, Edekabank AG developed an innovative financing concept to support customers to buy more efficient equipment and photovoltaic systems (Edeka, 2014a), Metro provided information to customers on the energy characteristics of different household appliances (Metro Group, 2008: 21–22; 2013a: 29) and all of the retailers offered a range of energy-efficient products (e.g. refrigerators, freezers, dishwashers, washing machines) (see, for example, Metro Group, 2008: 21–22, 2013a: 10; REWE Group, 2011: 80).

Wider reflections on governance processes in Germany

The German retail sector illustrates the sort of corporate responses that would be expected to be seen in a price-dominated market. Most of the actions taken are those that provide financially attractive returns, with actions that provide longer-term benefits less likely to be adopted. This has important implications for the governance processes that might be deployed in Germany. It suggests that companies are less likely to recognise or respond to external governance pressures unless these governance pressures have a direct impact on costs or are mandatory regulatory requirements. Expressed another way, in the absence of a dramatic shift in policy or regulation, German companies are unlikely to significantly alter their climate change strategies.

Interestingly, there is some evidence that German companies might change if they seek to expand internationally and need to compete in markets where corporate responsibility is a meaningful source of competitive advantage (or a potential source of commercial disadvantage). For example, both Aldi and Lidl placed much greater emphasis on product quality when they sought to expand in Switzerland, had to report on their energy-saving opportunities in Australia (under the Australian Energy Efficiency Obligation) and started to provide more information on their approach to corporate responsibility to support their growth strategies in the UK.

Finally, the German case-study points to the potential for corporate ownership to be an important determinant of corporate action. Metro, the only one of the five largest retailers that is publicly listed, identified pressure from investors for transparent communications on climate change, and investor interest in how the company manages climate-related risks and opportunities as important drivers for reporting and action (Metro Group, 2011b, 2012b). The other companies did not face this pressure. This lack of investor engagement provides a partial explanation for the lack of transparency by the unlisted companies.

France

Five retailers – Carrefour, ITM Enterprises, E. Leclerc, Groupe Auchan (Auchan) and Groupe Casino (Casino) – account for 60% by sales of the French grocery market (USDA, 2012). This section focuses on the four (Carrefour, E. Leclerc, Groupe Auchan (Auchan) and Groupe Casino (Casino)) which are ranked among the 25 largest global retailers (Deloitte, 2014).

External governance pressures: competing for attention

The perception of climate change among French retailers throughout the period 2000 to 2015 was that it was primarily a regulatory compliance (e.g. on CFCs, on product labelling) and operational cost issue, rather than a strategic value driver (Carrefour, 2012b; Groupe Auchan, 2014: 60). This perception did change in the period 2006–2008, when climate change started to be identified as one of the major sustainability challenges faced by both companies. From 2009, however, climate change reverted to being seen as an operational issue. There were various reasons for this perception: energy costs were a relatively small part of retailers' cost base, there was little direct pressure on the retailers to reduce their emissions (the pressures were much stronger on food producers), there was no overarching regulation of corporate entities, the other sustainability issues listed above were seen as much more pressing, and investors did not see climate change as a particularly important issue for the retail sector.

Climate change was also competing for attention with other sustainability issues. Most French retailers consistently identified their sustainability priorities as relating to supply chain management (e.g. traceability, quality and safety, the efficiency of natural resources consumption and usage, labour and human rights, and benefit sharing with smallholder farmers) and to food safety, health and nutrition. In relation to both supply chains and food, product-related regulation was the primary driver for action, with French retailers being required to implement significant new regulations on food labelling, health claims and the location of products in stores.

Internal governance processes: limited resources and competing agendas

Carrefour produced its first sustainability report in 2001 and Casino in 2003. Of the other two, Auchan only published its first formal external sustainable development report in 2012 and, by 2015, E. Leclerc had yet to provide a comprehensive account of its approach to corporate responsibility and sustainability.

While Carrefour, Casino and Auchan all provided information and data on their climate change and energy performance, it was difficult to assess overall

trends in performance across the sector. This reflected two distinct characteristics of their reporting. The first was that both Carrefour and Casino had, on a
number of occasions, restated their data, changed the scope of reporting and
changed their calculation methods. They had, however, provided limited
information on how these changes affected the numbers reported. The second
was that all of the companies emphasised efficiency and intensity measures
rather than absolute (or total) greenhouse gas emissions. In fact, neither Carrefour nor Auchan reported on their total greenhouse gas emissions in any of
their corporate responsibility reports; they only reported measures such as
energy use and/or greenhouse gas emissions per unit of floor sales area, and on
greenhouse gas emissions per pallet transported. Even where estimates of total
greenhouse gas emissions were provided (e.g. Casino reported on total emissions in its 2012 and 2013 sustainability reports; Carrefour reported total emissions in its CDP responses), there was limited information on whether the
numbers were comparable with previous years' data or on the factors that led
to changes in the reported numbers.

An important feature of the French retailers' internal governance processes was
that they had relatively limited internal resources for their corporate responsibility
and sustainability efforts. Most of these resources were focused on the sustainability
priorities discussed above (i.e. supply chain management, and food safety, health
and nutrition). This limited their ability to focus on other issues such as climate
change. It was not clear whether these limited resources were a cause or a consequence of the positioning of climate change as an operational rather than a strategic business issue. Interviewees did comment that it was difficult for French
retailers to increase their emphasis on climate change as this would compromise
the resources available for other sustainability-related areas.

Auchan, Carrefour and Casino adopted quite different approaches to their
climate change targets. In its 2011 Sustainable Development report, Auchan set
a target of reducing electricity consumption in its stores and shopping centres
by 2% in 2012 (Groupe Auchan, 2012: 29). However, in its 2013 sustainability
report, it did not publish an energy or climate change-related target (Groupe
Auchan, 2014). Carrefour's targets primarily related to improving the energy
and greenhouse gas emissions intensity of its operations. In 2007, it set a target
to reduce electricity consumption per square metre of sales floor area by 20%
over the period 2004 to 2015 (Carrefour, 2008: 3). In 2009, it changed this to
a 30% reduction over the period 2004 to 2020 (Carrefour, 2010a: 47, 68, 2014:
11). It subsequently supplemented this with a target to reduce greenhouse gas
emissions per square metre of sales floor area in France, Belgium, Spain and
Italy (representing 43% of the net sales of the group) by 40% over the period
2009 to 2020 (Carrefour, 2012b, 2014: 11). Over the period 2002–2006,
Casino's goals were primarily process-oriented (e.g. to test new technologies, to
improve control systems, to install more efficient equipment), with most being
of relatively short duration (one year ahead) and primarily focused on operations and transport (Groupe Casino, 2004: 12–13, 2005: 11, 2006: 15). Casino
subsequently started to set longer-term targets, with a greater focus on

greenhouse gas emissions. Among the most notable were to reduce emissions from the loss of refrigerants by 3% per annum between 2006 and 2010, to reduce greenhouse gas emissions from its French operations by 10% between 2004 and 2009, and to introduce a new environmental label on 100 Casino food products (Groupe Casino, 2006: 15; 2007: 9, 2008: 39, 43). In 2009, Casino made further long-term commitments, setting targets to reduce energy consumption per square metre by 2.5% per annum between 2009 and 2020, to reduce greenhouse gas emissions from refrigeration by 5% per annum between 2009 and 2020, to reduce greenhouse gas emissions from transport by 2% per unit annually between 2009 and 2020 and to expand the number of products covered by its carbon index (Groupe Casino, 2009: 11, 2010: 22, 2011: 80–81, 2012: 90).

Corporate responses: improving energy efficiency, supplier engagement and labelling

Reducing building and transport-related greenhouse gas emissions and improving energy consumption was a long-standing focus for all four of the retailers. In their buildings, they improved their monitoring of energy consumption, implemented energy management systems, improved building insulation, installed doors on refrigerators and freezers, improved the efficiency of lighting, heating, ventilation and air-conditioning systems, tested new refrigerants, installed photovoltaic and geothermal energy systems in a number of stores, provided training for staff, and incorporated environmental and energy considerations into new store design and operation (Carrefour, 2005: 38, 2009a: x, 2012a: 56, 2014: 11; Groupe Auchan, 2012: 29–33, 2014: 60–61; Groupe Casino, 2003: 23, 2007: 10–12, 2008: 17, 24, 2011: 58–59, 2013: 62–63, 2014: 68). In transport, all four consolidated transport routes, trialled alternative fuels, used cleaner vehicles, optimised logistics and used alternative methods of transport (such as rivers and railways) (see, for example, Carrefour, 2005: 34–35, 2012a: 56; Groupe Auchan, 2012: 3, 18, 2014: 45; Groupe Casino, 2003: 26–27, 2007: 12–13, 2011: 58–59).

The French retailers provided limited information on their investments in energy efficiency and renewable energy. The exception was Carrefour, which reported that it had invested approximately 30 million euros a year in energy efficiency between 2009 and 2012 (Carrefour, 2009a: x, 2012b). Carrefour also provided some interesting insights into its investment criteria. In its 2012 response to the CDP, it stated that investments in on-site renewable energy offered payback periods of eight years (in a best-case scenario). It commented that it considered it more economically and environmentally efficient to focus on energy efficiency (Carrefour, 2012b; see also, Carrefour, 2009a: x).

The actions taken by the French retailers enabled them to consistently, year on year, improve their emissions and energy intensity (per unit of floor area or per unit of product transported). For example, over the period 2009 to 2013, Carrefour reduced the greenhouse gas emissions associated with store energy consumption per unit of sales area by 26.7% compared to 2009 (Carrefour, 2014: 67), a rate of improvement of approximately 7.5% per annum. Over the same period, the average electricity consumption per unit of floor area in Auchan's hypermarkets improved by approximately 3.5% per annum (Groupe Auchan, 2012: 32, 2014; 78). In relation to transport, Casino reduced the greenhouse gas emissions per pallet transported by an average of 2.5% per annum between 2004 and 2009, and Carrefour reported that its emissions per pallet transported had remained broadly stable over the period 2010 to 2013 (Carrefour, 2014: 67). As discussed above, despite the improvements in energy efficiency and greenhouse gas emissions intensity, it is not possible to offer a definitive view on trends in overall greenhouse gas emissions from the sector, although it is likely that business growth and changes in business models (e.g. increased sales of refrigerated and frozen products) exerted upward pressure on energy consumption and greenhouse gas emissions. This was acknowledged by Carrefour in its 2012 CDP response when it noted that, because of new store openings, its energy and greenhouse gas emission reduction efforts would not necessarily result in a decrease in its absolute emissions (Carrefour, 2012b).

The French retailers took a variety of actions to reduce emissions from their supply chains. The most common action was to shorten transport distances, although this was primarily driven by French consumers' expectations on local sourcing with any reductions in greenhouse gas emissions being a secondary benefit. The retailers also worked with their suppliers to improve their energy efficiency and reduce their emissions. For example, Carrefour provided suppliers with an online self-assessment tool, supported suppliers with the development of action plans, and organised supplier workshops (Carrefour, 2010a: 63–64, 2010b, 2011: 63, 2012b). However, none of the retailers provided information on whether these activities led to reductions in their suppliers' greenhouse gas emission reduction efforts. In practice, there was limited scrutiny of suppliers' climate change performance and little active engagement to encourage emission reductions.

Casino was the only retailer to have adopted carbon labelling. It created a carbon label in mid-2008, and extended this to a wider environmental label (covering greenhouse gas emissions, water consumption and water pollution) in 2011 (Groupe Casino, 2008: 10, 2012: 72). Over 680 products displayed the Casino carbon index or the Casino environmental index by the end of 2011 (Groupe Casino, 2012: 72). Carrefour consistently opposed carbon labelling, arguing that such labels were confusing for customers (see, for example, Carrefour, 2008: 15, 2009b: 15, 2011: 124, 134)). Carrefour argued that a life-cycle approach was a more appropriate approach, as it would allow greater understanding of the different environmental impacts across the whole life-cycle and thereby enable efficient targeted action on the greatest impacts (Carrefour, 2010b). Carrefour conducted life-cycle assessments on checkout bags, catalogues, packaging and various food products and used this analysis to inform customers on how to reduce emissions (e.g. through modifying cooking and washing guidelines) (Carrefour, 2010b, 2012a).

The retailers also engaged with their customers on environmental and related issues. For example, Auchan held 'Green Days' at its hypermarkets and super-markets, with a focus on planting trees and encouraging environmentally friendly modes of transport (Groupe Auchan, 2012: 3, 35), and Carrefour participated in European Sustainable Energy Week and Earth Hour (Carrefour, 2009a: xi, 2009b: 15, 2010a: 47, 2011: 130–131, 2013: 23). They also offered products that would help their customers reduce their energy consumption (e.g. solar mobile chargers, standby cut-off plugs for electrical appliances, home insulation, low-energy light bulbs) (Carrefour, 2007: 6, 2009a: xi, 2010b, 2011: 128, 2012b).

Wider reflections on governance processes in France

In a similar manner to the German retail case-study, the French retail case-study shows how external governance pressures, in this case on climate change, can be crowded out by other external pressures. The difference is that in Germany it was the emphasis on financially attractive returns that meant that other external governance pressures were less likely to have an effect, whereas in France it was that other sustainability issues were seen as much more important.

The French case-study also shows how internal governance conditions can exacerbate this problem. The fact that other sustainability issues are perceived by companies as being of greater importance than climate change, compounded by climate change being seen as an operational rather than a strategic issue and by the limited internal resources available for climate change-related activities, meant that the governance context could be described as relatively weak external pressures looking to influence relatively unresponsive organisations. The consequence was, unsurprisingly, that the actions taken by the retailers were relatively modest. Even though there was a short period where the external pressures for action were relatively strong, the lack of strong internal governance processes meant that these strong external pressures did not drive substantial or sustained changes in corporate practice. This was seen with both Carrefour and Casino, both of whom identified climate change as one of their major sustainability challenges in the period 2006 to 2008. By 2009, however, climate change was being presented as one part of Carrefour's actions to improve its overall environmental performance. While Casino did maintain its emphasis on climate change through to 2011, by 2012 it too had started to place greater emphasis on wider environmental management, with climate change just one part of this.

There are three other points that are worth highlighting about this case-study. The first is the corporate framing of climate change as an operational and efficiency issue means that external governance pressures that seek to encourage a wider focus or a focus on absolute performance are less likely to be recognised as legitimate by the corporation. The second is that corporate framing is self-perpetuating. Once a particular approach is seen as 'the way to do things', it is much harder to challenge the legitimacy or credibility of the approach and, therefore, it is harder to demand further action. The third is that ownership, as we also noted in the case of Germany, does seem to be an important influence on internal governance processes. This is seen most clearly in relation to reporting where the two publicly listed companies, Carrefour and Casino, produced their first sustainability reports in 2001 and Casino in 2003. In contrast, Auchan only published its first sustainable development report in 2012 and E. Leclerc had not published such a report by 2015.

Australia

In this section, we focus on Coles and Woolworths, the two Australian retailers in the list of the top 25 global retailers by turnover (Deloitte, 2014: G12). Together, these companies accounted for 78% of the Australian supermarket share in 2009, and for 50 to 70% of total food and grocery industry sales across most product categories (Australian Food and Grocery Council and A.T. Kearney Australia, 2011: 1, 4, 13).

External governance pressures: the oscillating politics of climate change

The dependence of the Australian economy on the mining and minerals industries – the minerals resources industry accounted for more than 8% of GDP and over half of total exports of goods and services (Australian Bureau of Statistics, 2012) – and on relatively low-cost energy have been a huge influence on climate change policy in Australia and, in turn, on Australian corporate responses to climate change. In the period 2000 to 2015, understanding the politics of climate change (and the politics of mining and energy) is central to understanding the external governance pressures on Australian retailers.

Despite being one of the few countries permitted to increase its greenhouse gas emissions under the Kyoto Protocol – Australia was required to cap its greenhouse gas emissions at 108% of its 1990 emissions, to be achieved on an annual basis over the five years from 2008 to 2012 – the Australian government did not ratify the Kyoto Protocol. Its argument was that the Protocol did not provide a clear pathway for emission reduction actions by developing countries, and would therefore disadvantage Australian industry. The importance of not threatening or damaging Australia's international competitiveness was an explicit goal of Australia's climate change policies through to the mid-2000s (see, for example, the 1997 statement by the then Prime Minister John Howard [Howard, 1997]). The government relied primarily on relatively weak voluntary measures to encourage business action on climate change (Sullivan, 2005: 97–131, 2006, 2007, 2008: 100–116).

Since the mid-2000s, climate change has been one of the defining political issues in Australia, and played a major role in each of the 2007, 2010 and 2013 elections. In 2006, Al Gore's film, *An Inconvenient Truth*, was released in Australia, coinciding with the eighth consecutive year of drought in Australia and the fourth consecutive term of the Liberal/National government. In the 2007 election campaign, the opposition Labor Party's core election pledges included the ratification of the Kyoto Protocol and the establishment of a national emissions trading scheme. In November 2007, Labor was elected with a large majority and in December 2007 Australia ratified the Kyoto Protocol.

In late 2008, Labor announced the details of a Carbon Pollution Reduction Scheme (CPRS), effectively a cap-and-trade scheme, which would cut Australia's greenhouse gas emissions by at least 5% by 2020 against a 2000 baseline. The proposals faced strong opposition from industry groups – particularly the Minerals Council of Australia – and were voted down in Parliament in August 2009. Despite efforts to broker an agreement with the opposition Liberal Party, the CPRS was subsequently voted down in Parliament for a second time. In April 2010, Labor put the proposals for an emissions trading scheme on hold until at least 2013.

The 2010 election saw Labor retain power, albeit as a minority government relying on the support of one Green Party and three independent Members of Parliament. In November 2011, a comprehensive package of climate change measures, The Clean Energy Future legislation, was passed by the Senate. These measures included the establishment of a carbon price scheme, the linking of Australia's emissions trading scheme to international emissions trading schemes, the adoption of a target to reduce Australia's emissions by 5% from 2000 levels by 2020, generous industry assistance to compensate for the impacts of the carbon tax, the closure of some existing coal-fired power stations and the provision of significant financial support for renewable energy (Commonwealth of Australia, 2011). The carbon price scheme began on 1 July 2012 and raised $3.8 billion in its first six months. However, the Treasury predicted that, because of falls in international carbon prices, revenues from the carbon tax would drop by $6 billion over the next four years. This prediction led to the government deferring $2.8 billion in tax cuts it had planned for 2015 (Lane, 2013). In July 2013, the Labor government announced that it would terminate the carbon tax and instead look to establish an emissions trading scheme.

In September 2013, the Liberal/National coalition won the Federal election. One of the core elements of its campaign manifesto was the repeal of much of Australia's climate change-related legislation. In July 2014, the Australian government voted to disband the entire package of climate change measures.

Apart from politics, the other important influence on corporate action on climate change was energy prices. Historically, Australian electricity prices were relatively low compared to other countries. In fact, various studies suggested that the rate of improvement in end-use energy efficiency in Australia from 1990 to the early 2000s was about half the OECD average (Commonwealth of Australia, 2004). After remaining broadly constant in real terms over the period 2002 to 2007, electricity prices rose by approximately 40% in the period from 2007 to 2012 (Carbon + Energy Markets, 2012). This rise was compounded by the strengthening of the Australian dollar, which meant that energy prices became an increasingly important issue for exporters. It is, however, relevant to note that, notwithstanding these increases, electricity prices in Australia had only reached the point where they were broadly comparable with those in other OECD countries (Carbon + Energy Markets, 2012; ESAA, 2012).

Internal governance processes: well developed but focused on buildings and transport

Woolworths produced its first corporate responsibility report in 2005, and reported to the CDP (previously the Carbon Disclosure project) from 2007. Woolworths also published information on its approach to energy management under the Australian Energy Efficiency Opportunities Act (which, until its repeal in 2014, required companies to implement energy efficiency opportunities with a payback period of less than four years). In 2007, Coles was taken over by Wesfarmers, an Australian-listed company with interests in retail, insurance, resources and mining, energy, chemicals and fertilisers, and industrial and safety supplies. Since then, Wesfarmers has provided information on Coles' approach to climate change and energy management, as part of its sustainability reporting, in its reporting to the CDP and in its reporting under the Australian Energy Efficiency Opportunities Act.

Climate change was seen by both Coles and Woolworths as an issue that they needed to manage and understand, in particular in relation to their operations (buildings and transport). The importance assigned to managing their operational emissions was driven by rising energy prices, the likelihood of future climate change and energy-related legislation, and emissions reporting requirements. Both companies identified two other drivers for action: their employees saw action on climate change as important and their company leaders and senior management were aware of the importance of effective action on climate change as an integral part of growing successful and sustainable businesses over the longer term.

Coles and Woolworths had very different approaches to setting and reporting on targets. The Wesfarmers approach, which applied to all aspects of its business not just sustainability, was to rarely provide targets for profits, dividends or other financial issues. Its approach was to develop and implement strategies to achieve internal goals, which would then be reflected in its performance (Wesfarmers, 2013: 5). In contrast, Woolworths did publish targets. In its 2007–2015 Sustainability Strategy, it committed to stabilising its facility-related greenhouse gas emissions at 2007 levels by 2015 (representing a 40% reduction compared to business-as-usual emissions), reducing greenhouse gas emissions per square metre by 25% for new sustainable store designs compared with business-as-usual designs, reducing greenhouse gas emissions per carton delivered by Woolworths-owned trucks by 25% by 2012, and reducing greenhouse gas emissions from its company car fleet by 30% by 2010 (Woolworths, 2007: 2–4, 14–16).

Both companies allocated capital for energy efficiency, although these investments were expected to achieve rates of return that were comparable with other business-related investments. Over the period 2009 to 2012, Coles invested over A$100 million in energy efficiency, with expected payback periods for these investments typically between one and three years (Wesfarmers, 2012b). Similarly, Woolworths noted that the 37 energy and climate change-related projects that it commenced in FY2011 were expected to provide an average payback period of 3.1 years (Woolworths, 2012b).

Corporate responses: reducing operational emissions

Both Coles and Woolworths made significant efforts to reduce their operational emissions and improve energy efficiency. They installed energy-efficient lighting, improved their monitoring and management of equipment and energy use, improved energy control systems, installed glass fronts and lids on refrigeration and freezer units, recovered and reused waste heat, increased staff awareness and encouraged practices such as switching off lights, air-conditioning units and exhaust fans when not in use, adopted sustainability standards for new buildings, and installed new energy efficiency heating, lighting, air-conditioning and refrigeration equipment (Wesfarmers, 2009: 28, 2010: 32, 2011: 21, 29, 2012a: 22; Woolworths, 2005: 5, 2007: 14, 2008: 70, 2009: 54, 2010: 48–51, 2011a: 28). They reduced their transport-related emissions through introducing more energy-efficient and lower-emitting vehicles, improving logistics and planning, using larger and fuller containers, consolidating transport routes and working with transport suppliers (Coles, 2014; Woolworths, 2005: 5, 2007: 16, 2009: 54, 2010: 51, 2011a: 30).

As a result of these efforts, Coles reduced its operational (Scope 1 and Scope 2) emissions by 12% over the period 2010 to 2013 (i.e. an annual improvement of approximately 4% per annum) (Wesfarmers, 2013: 46). If emissions from waste disposal and air travel are included, Coles' total emissions reduced by 22% over the period 2008 to 2013 (i.e. by approximately 5% per annum) (Wesfarmers, 2012a: 6, 2013: 46). Woolworths' operational, waste and transport-related emissions remained broadly stable over the period 2008 to 2013, although its emissions intensity (expressed in terms of greenhouse gas emissions per unit of turnover) declined by 14% over the period 2009 to 2013 (Woolworths, 2008: 68, 2009: 53–55, 2010: 50, 2011a: 29, 2012a: 37, 2013: 34, 41). Woolworths noted that a variety of factors affected its emissions profile; these included the move towards larger stores, the growth in demand for refrigerated convenience meals, the increase in the number of cars in its fleet, delays in converting to more fuel-efficient cars, the lead time between measures being implemented and changes being seen in the company's emissions profile, and business growth (Woolworths, 2008: 68–72, 2009: 54, 2010: 48). Woolworths also highlighted the lack of meaningful incentives for renewable energy adoption and the uncertainties about the direction of policy as contributory factors (see, for example, Woolworths, 2007: 14, 2010: 4).

Neither company provided much information on their approach to reducing emissions from their supply chains. In discussions, they confirmed that they provided some technical support to smaller suppliers (e.g. providing them with guidance on energy-related issues when they are planning on new investments). However, both companies were clear that reducing operational emissions was their main priority, and that they had limited resources for working with suppliers.

Both companies made supportive statements on the need for effective policy action on climate change. For example, Wesfarmers supported carbon pricing as a means of reducing emissions over time, although it also argued that this should be introduced gradually to allow companies time to adapt (Wesfarmers, 2012a: 2). These progressive views were somewhat at odds with the views expressed by a number of the retail industry bodies of which Coles and Woolworths are members; for example, the Australian Food and Grocery Council, the Australian National Retailers' Association and the Australian Retailers Association all lobbied for the repeal of carbon tax legislation (AFGC, 2014; ANRA 2014; ARA 2014).

The interactions between external governance pressures, internal governance conditions and corporate responses

The Australian experience illustrates the kind of responses and actions that might be seen when external pressures oscillate in a relatively unpredictable manner. It leads to companies focusing on those issues where the financial case for action is clearest and where the payback periods are relatively short. One of the interesting features of the decisions made by both companies was that they concentrated most of their efforts on those areas where there was a clear financial case for action, i.e. where the benefits outweighed the costs in the absence of carbon prices or carbon taxes. That is not to say that they did not also look at the effects of carbon prices or carbon taxes when making investment decisions (Wesfarmers, 2012b) but they were clear that investment decisions needed to be able to meet internal target rates of return without carbon-related incentives. This has important implications for policymakers as it means that carbon taxes or other financial instruments need to be set at a higher level or run for a longer period to overcome the perceived credibility gap in government policy (this issue, including analysis of the Australian political context, is discussed in Sullivan, 2011b).

The Australian case-study also highlights the importance of energy and carbon prices. Energy efficiency was a lower priority for Australian corporates through to the mid-2000s, reflecting the low energy prices that prevailed in Australia at that time, as well as the perception that energy costs were just a cost of doing business. This changed as a result of the significant rise in Australian energy prices from 2007 onwards, reinforced by the expectation that policy measures such as emissions trading and the carbon tax would have a direct effect on electricity prices (Woolworths 2007: 12–14, 2008: 66–67, 2009: 52, 2011a: 28; Wesfarmers, 2013: 3).

In their corporate responsibility reports, both Coles and Woolworths identified customer expectations as an important driver for action, with reducing greenhouse gas emissions increasingly seen as a business-as-usual expectation of large companies (see, for example, Woolworths, 2007: 12, 2009: 52). However, as we have seen in the other case-studies, there was a significant gap between consumers' intentions and action. For example, a 2008 survey of Australian consumer attitudes to climate change (partly sponsored by Woolworths) found that a majority were concerned about climate change and were trying to conserve energy at home. However, Woolworths noted that its sales data found a major gap between consumer attitudes and behaviour; it noted that consumers were making purchasing choices based on factors such as utility, quality, value and health, and not just environmental attributes (Woolworths, 2008: 75). Similarly, a 2010 Green Shopper Survey found that while 93% of customers thought that a retailer's effort to reduce its environmental impact was important, only 13% of those surveyed had actually bought a 'green' product (Woolworths, 2011b). These findings were confirmed by a 2013 survey which found that, while 80% of the survey respondents thought that climate change was happening and could be attributable to human activity, climate change ranked low in importance when compared to other concerns; in fact, climate change was ranked as the 14th most important concern among 16 general concerns, and seventh out of eight environmental concerns (Leviston et al., 2014).

Concluding comments

The international case-studies confirm the broad conclusions from the UK supermarket sector case-study. They confirm that weak external pressures can, if they are aligned, have a significant influence on internal governance processes and on corporate strategies and actions. They confirm that internal governance processes strongly influence the responsiveness of organisations to external pressures and the degree to which companies institutionalise their responses to these pressures within their businesses. They confirm the critical importance of the business case for action; there is limited evidence that companies will invest capital in situations where the financial costs outweigh the financial benefits of such investments. They confirm that external pressures, internal governance conditions and corporate responses interact with and influence each other, and that it is therefore important to analyse these as a dynamic, interactive system rather than analysing each in isolation.

The international case-studies also deepen our understanding of governance processes, providing six additional insights to those presented at the start of this chapter. First, the details of the business context – for example, economic conditions, market structure (e.g. the relationship with suppliers), market drivers (e.g. do retailers compete on the basis of price, brand, sustainability, or other factors), corporate and business cultures (e.g. is there a culture of leadership or conformance, is there a culture of collaboration with sector peers or with other actors such as government) – influence the specific actions that are taken by companies.

Second, at the individual firm, corporate ownership is important. There is some evidence that publicly listed companies are more likely to be more transparent about their climate change practices, processes and performance, although it is not possible to say whether they are actually better performers.

Third, companies have strikingly similar investment decision-making criteria. Financial factors (i.e. costs and benefits) dominate decision-making, investments are generally expected to pay for themselves within three years, and – acknowledging that some companies do have specific budgets for energy-related investments – climate change and energy-related investments are competing for capital with other projects. It is important to clarify this latter point as it does not necessarily mean that there is a level playing field for climate change-related investments. The reality is that, in the absence of an explicit preference for climate change or energy-related investments, companies tend to prefer investments that enable business growth. This is seen in the way in which the UK retail companies approach innovation. The emphasis on adopting new technologies at the point when stores and other infrastructure are being built or upgraded, while offering advantages from economic and practical perspectives, also provides a clear message around priorities as it is the rate of store build or refurbishment that drives the rate of adoption of energy-saving or emission reduction technologies.

Fourth, the effect of external governance pressures depends not only on the strength of these pressures (with the alignment of these pressures being particularly important), but also on the duration of these pressures, the dependability (and perceived dependability) of these pressures, and the other, non-climate change-related, pressures faced by companies. In relation to duration, a number of the case-studies suggest that pressures need to be sustained for a number of years in order for companies to develop their internal governance processes (their systems and their management views on the strategic importance of climate change). If pressures are not sustained or not seen as long-term features of the business landscape, companies do not shift from a view that climate change is primarily an operational issue. In relation to other pressures, if the situation is one where other pressures dominate business thinking or where companies need to respond to multiple sustainability-related pressures, climate change pressures need to be much stronger and of longer duration to have an effect on internal governance processes and corporate responses.

Fifth, the quality of internal governance processes is important. If management systems and processes are not well developed or if management sees climate change as an operational issue, internal governance processes will tend to attenuate or dampen the influence of external pressures. Conversely, well-developed and responsive management systems and processes and a management recognition of climate change as a strategic value driver means that companies are more likely to respond effectively and quickly to external governance pressures. While internal governance processes are important in institutionalising and ensuring the longevity of corporate actions on climate change, they can only play this role for a limited time in the absence of external governance pressures. Without ongoing external drivers for action, climate change inevitably loses some of its importance and, as we have seen in some of the case-studies, reverts to being seen as an issue of business efficiency and cost reduction.

Sixth, the actions taken by companies depend on both external governance pressures and internal governance processes. The weaker the external pressures or the less developed the internal governance processes, the more likely it is that companies will set less ambitious objectives, either in terms of the greenhouse gas emissions that they seek to achieve or in terms of the urgency with which they look to take action. Companies are not passive actors, and there is not a linear relationship between external pressures and corporate action. Companies can shape and influence these external pressures, and the UK and international case-studies present a number of examples. For example, corporate disclosures generally do not allow meaningful comparisons to be made between companies and often make it difficult to tell how well companies are performing against their own targets. Another example is how corporate reporting can be used by companies to frame debates in terms that suit their own interests, e.g. to present their performance in the best light, to emphasise relative (or efficiency) rather than absolute performance, to emphasise operational performance rather than wider supply chain and value chain-related impacts.

Supplementary information

Table 5.2 US retailers' overarching climate change commitments (as at 1 June 2014)

Company	Overarching commitments
Amazon.com	• No published targets.
Best Buy	• Reduce US carbon footprint by 20% by the year 2020 (over a 2009 baseline) (Best Buy, 2013: 47, 2014: 7).
Costco	• No emission reduction target (Costco, 2012b).
CVS Caremark	• Reduce total Scope 1 and Scope 2 emissions per square foot of floor area by 15% over the period 2010 to 2018 (CVS Caremark, 2014: 35).
Home Depot	• Reduce GHG emissions from upstream transportation and distribution by 20% by 2015 against a 2009 baseline (Home Depot, 2014: 8). • Reduce electricity per square foot in US stores by 20% by 2015 against a 2004 baseline (Home Depot, 2014: 8).
Kroger	• No published targets (Note 1).
Lowe's	• Improve energy efficiency by 13% per square foot over the period 2010 to 2010 (Lowe's, 2014: 54). • Reduce carbon emissions by 20% per square foot over the period 2010 to 2020 (Lowe's, 2014: 54).

(continued)

Table 5.2 *(continued)*

Company	Overarching commitments
Safeway	• Reduce absolute greenhouse gas emissions by 20% by 2020 against a 2010 baseline (Safeway, 2014).
Target	• Reduce total Scope 1 and Scope 2 emissions (in te CO_2e) per square foot by 10% by 2016 against a 2007 baseline (Target, 2014). • Reduce total Scope 1 and Scope 2 emissions (in te CO_2e) per unit revenue 20% by 2016 against a 2007 baseline (Target, 2014).
Walgreens	• No published targets.
Walmart	• Reduce total Scope 1 and 2 emissions from buildings by 20% by 2020, against a 2010 baseline (Walmart, 2014: 86, 91). • Eliminate 20 million tonnes of GHG emissions from the life-cycle of the products Walmart sells by 2015 (Walmart, 2014: 101). • Be supplied 100% by renewable energy (although a target year for this goal has not been specified) (Walmart, 2014: 86). • Double fleet efficiency (i.e. double the number of cases shipped per unit of fuel used) in the United States by 2015, against a 2005 baseline (Walmart, 2014: 86).

Note: While Kroger's 2014 Sustainability Report (Kroger, 2014) did not include any climate change-related targets, Kroger had previously set targets to improve its truck fleet efficiency by 40% by 2014 against a 2008 baseline and to reduce stores' overall energy use by 35% by 2013 against a 2000 baseline (Kroger, 2012b: 31, 32).

Table 5.3 Trends in greenhouse gas emissions for US retailers

Company	Annual change in greenhouse gas emissions (%/year)
Best Buy	−4.11 (over 4 years)
Costco	+4.40 (4 years)
CVS Caremark	−0.67 (4 years)
Home Depot	−6.29 (4 years)
Kroger	−0.10 (7 years)
Lowe's	−1.98 (4 years)
Target	+1.76 (4 years)
Walmart	+1.71 (6 years)

Sources: Best Buy (2014); Costco, 2012a); CVS Caremark (2012, 2013, 2014); Home Depot (2014); Kroger (2012a, 2014); Lowe's (2012); Target (2014); Walmart (2014).

Table 5.4 Projected changes in US retailers' greenhouse gas emissions

Company	Expected changes in greenhouse gas emissions
CVS Caremark	• CVS Caremark notes that it is in growth mode, and constantly building new pharmacy stores, distribution centres and office facilities. It therefore expects its absolute emissions to gradually rise over time and is investing in changes to prevent them from growing at the same rate as its square footage (CVS Caremark, 2014: 35).
Home Depot	• Absolute GHG emissions from US stores are expected to reduce by 8% over the period 2011 to 2015, assuming that Home Depot's retail floor does not change substantially over this period (Home Depot, 2012).
Lowe's	• Scope 1 emissions expected to vary in proportion to the organic growth of the company (Lowe's, 2012). • Scope 2 emissions expected to increase but Scope 2 emissions per unit of retail floor space expected to reduce by up to 3% per annum for the period 2012–2017 (Lowe's, 2012).
Target	• Absolute GHG emissions are expected to increase through to 2016 (Target, 2014).
Walmart	• Walmart expects to hold its total Scope 1 and 2 emissions flat over the period 2010 to 2020 (Walmart, 2014: 84).

6 Designing and deploying effective internal and external governance processes

The case-studies in Chapters 4 and 5 explained how, between 2000 and 2015, external governance pressures and international governance conditions coincided to affect the climate change strategies and responses of firms within the retail sector. This analysis allows us to draw some conclusions about which external governance pressures and internal governance conditions were the most important influences on the sector, and about the characteristics of these conditions that affected their level of influence. In this chapter, we take the insights from the case-study chapters and use them to draw wider conclusions about how corporate practice and performance might be shaped by these governance processes, and about how these governance processes might be harnessed to shape and influence corporate practice and performance.

We begin this chapter by focusing on how one particular stakeholder group, consumers, has influenced corporate strategy and performance. In this analysis we consolidate the insights on consumers and the retail sector from the case-study chapters. We describe the emergence of consumer interest in climate change, the intensity of this pressure, how these pressures have been perceived by retailers and how retailers have responded. We then open out our discussion to consider in more general terms the governance processes that influence corporate practice and performance, the manner in which these have been deployed in the retail sector and the conclusions that may be drawn about their future deployment.

Case-study: consumers

What issues are consumers concerned about?

Many retailers, both in their interviews with us and in their corporate responsibility reports, pointed to the 1990s as the time when general issues of corporate responsibility appeared on the consumer agenda, and the early to mid-2000s as the point when climate change first started to receive more consumer attention. They commented that the subjects of consumer interest and the level of consumer interest in these issues are strongly influenced by the media and NGO campaigns, with the level of interest changing – rising and falling rather than moving in a constant direction – over time. The UK provides a good illustration of this. From 2002 to 2005, the issues that were of concern to consumers included being a good employer, ethical trading, responsible use of technology, use of sustainable raw materials, and animal welfare. The period 2005 to 2007, which corresponded to a peak in media and societal interest in climate change, saw climate change (in particular, reducing energy use) and waste receiving much greater attention. By 2009 and 2010, the issues of concern had changed again, with retailers identifying the carbon impact of suppliers, nutritional value of food and responsible sourcing as important issues for consumers. But consumer interest in climate change was not sustained; in a 2013 survey, Sainsbury's customers ranked its carbon footprint as the 14th, out of a list of 22, most important corporate responsibility issues (J Sainsbury, 2013: 9).

Furthermore, not only is climate change just one of a variety of social, environmental and ethical issues of concern to consumers, but social and environmental issues themselves are just one of a whole series of issues of concern to consumers. Consumer surveys consistently suggest that factors such as price, quality, service, product availability and store location are widely seen as much more important than corporate social and environmental performance in determining whether or not consumers will decide to shop at a particular retailer. Expressed another way, when we think about consumers and climate change, we need to recognise that we are talking about an issue that is effectively a subset of a subset of the issues that might be of concern.

Do consumers who are concerned about climate change actually act on that concern?

The evidence across all of the countries studied is that, despite the level of attention paid by the media and corporate responsibility reports to climate change, consumers have actually paid little attention to the retailers' climate change strategies. There are various reasons for this. First, as noted above, climate change is just one of many issues of concern to consumers; relatively few people make climate change the sole or primary determinant of where they shop. Second, consumers lack the capacity or understanding of how corporations work to exert influence in a targeted or effective way. Third, the transparency and accountability processes that do exist do not work for consumers. While many retailers have set targets and report on their performance, the quality of the data being reported and the manner in which these data are reported make it very difficult for consumers to determine whether the corporate commitments are serious and meaningful, whether companies are complying with these commitments or whether a particular company is a better or worse performer. Fourth, consumers are rarely able to articulate the specific expectations that they have of supermarkets. The reality is that consumers have limited choice other than to simply assume that retailers do a reasonable job of managing the issue in question. The retailers' responses – their management systems and processes, the actions they have taken, their communications – are, at least in part, directed at reassuring consumers that this assumption is justified.

A slightly different picture emerges when we look at consumer purchasing practices. Many of the retailers, in their corporate responsibility reports and reports to the CDP, agreed that a significant subset of their customers – even in the highly price-sensitive German market – that would preferentially purchase products with better environmental characteristics. This is most obvious in relation to electrical goods. For these goods, running costs (i.e. electricity consumption) can be an important part of the overall cost to the consumer, and most countries now have well-developed, credible energy efficiency labelling schemes (e.g. the US Energy Star scheme; the A to G rating system used in Europe). Many of the retailers also identified and targeted markets for products that were seen as better for the environment (e.g. low-energy lightbulbs) and for services and advice linked to these products (e.g. advice on home insulation).

Despite the high level of marketing support for these products, many retailers saw the market for 'climate friendly' products as being relatively limited, other than in situations where government regulated to ban or limit access to particular products (e.g. traditional tungsten filament lightbulbs). Consumers proved reluctant to pay more for products with environmentally desirable characteristics, and struggled to make informed decisions unless information was presented in very simple and credible terms (e.g. A–G energy labelling). The retailers' experience with product labelling (or carbon footprinting) provides some interesting insights into reasons why. As discussed in Chapters 4 and 5, some retailers developed carbon labels for some of their products, and actively promoted these labels to their customers. Yet, carbon labelling had not, by 2015, been widely adopted in any of the markets studied. Perhaps the most obvious reason was that there was no standard carbon label (in contrast to electrical goods where product labels were widely recognised and understood by consumers). For reasons of brand and differentiation, retailers preferred to develop their own labelling schemes and to apply them to their own products. This meant that consumers could not compare carbon-labelled products from different retailers. Comparability was only part of the problem. For labelled products, the carbon footprint was often just one part of the information being provided; the packaging for food products often also provided ingredient-related information, nutrition-related information and packaging-related information. In addition to the issues with presenting and communicating carbon labels to consumers, the practical challenges included the cost of conducting the assessments, the costs of the labelling process, concerns about whether customers would actually use the information provided, the complexity of labelling (with labels needing to be revised if there are any changes in the supply chain), and the risk of being accused of over-simplification by reducing environmental impact to a single number.

Retailers, across all of the markets studied, recognised the significant gap between consumers' intent and action. While many, or even a majority in certain surveys at certain times, of consumers expressed concern about climate change, their decisions on where to shop and what to purchase were based primarily on factors such as convenience, quality, value and health. Despite the apparent weaknesses in consumer pressure for the retailers to take action on climate change, many of the retailers pointed to consumer demand as a primary reason for them to take action on climate change. This is not simply a case of the retailers misreading or misinterpreting the strength or dependability of the signals being sent by customers. In fact, the retailers, both in our interviews with them and in their corporate responsibility reports, were consistent in acknowledging that the pressures from consumers were extremely weak, even in the period 2005 to 2007. However, they were of the view that they needed to be prepared for a strengthening of consumer pressures, seeing taking action on greenhouse gas emissions or 'being responsible' as 'a business-as-usual expectation of large companies'. They also pointed to the extreme competition that characterised – and continues to characterise – the sector, with every gain or loss of customers having a direct impact on cashflows and profits. The consequence is that retailers are very sensitive to anything that may attract new customers or cause customers to shop elsewhere, and it means that they see pre-empting or proactively anticipating the issues that are of concern or interest to their customers as being of huge commercial importance.

The retailers, as we discussed in Chapters 4 and 5, defined their climate change responsibilities in different ways. All sought to improve energy efficiency in their own operations and, to the extent that their customers were interested, to offer energy-efficient products (e.g. low-energy lightbulbs) and services. Beyond that, the responses varied, driven by wider market and sectoral pressures. For example, UK retailers worked with their agricultural suppliers to reduce energy consumption and greenhouse gas emissions; these efforts were not only motivated by concerns about climate change but also by the need to respond to consumer concern about the relationship between retailers and their suppliers, and the desire to reduce the cost of these products. In contrast, Japanese retailers encouraged customers to purchase offsets, using this as a means of customer engagement. Many retailers, including those in the UK and Japan, sought to educate their customers about climate change and about the financial and other benefits of using energy-efficient equipment, and have offered incentives to purchase energy-efficient products. These efforts were seen as providing a series of business benefits, e.g. they allowed retailers to sell more environmental or 'green' products; they allowed retailers to develop better and deeper relationships with their customers; they provided a positive green halo for the corporate brand.

In interviews, retailers commented that they needed to be careful about how they approached their engagement with their customers on climate change and other environmental issues. They cautioned that there were business risks associated with being too far ahead of their customers' expectations, of focusing on issues that were not seen as important by their customers, of offering products that customers are unwilling to buy (either because of price or because the characteristics of the product were inferior to less environmentally friendly products) and of potential inconsistencies between the corporate branding and corporate practice on climate change.

While not discussed explicitly by interviewees, it is clear that the retailers' climate change strategies have played an important role in limiting or deflecting the pressure that might have been exerted by customers. The quality of the information provided by retailers did limit customers' ability to meaningfully compare retailers or to hold retailers to account for their climate change performance. This information was used by many of the retailers to frame climate change as an issue of corporate energy efficiency and carbon efficiency rather than absolute emission reductions, and as an issue where retailers should focus on direct (or operational) emissions rather than supply chain related emissions. Unsurprisingly, the retailers paid little attention to the role that reduced consumption might play in society's response to climate change.

Governance from the outside

Where do governance pressures come from and what stops them emerging?

The evidence from the retail sector suggests that external governance pressures are most likely to emerge when there is an issue of concern to stakeholders (e.g. consumers, NGOs, the media, investors), when the actors (in this case, companies) have a causal role in the creation of the problem and/or a potential contribution to make to the solution, and when these stakeholders see that they can influence the actions of the actor in question. The emergence of these external governance pressures also depends on the actions being taken, whether the wider policy environment is supportive of stakeholder action and whether there are tools or mechanisms that enable the stakeholders to act or exert influence. The converse to all of these conditions also applies; stakeholders are less likely to exert pressure if they do not see the issue as being of concern, if they do not see that they have a role to play, if the relevant actors (i.e. companies) are already taking action or if there are significant barriers to action.

Climate change has been an issue of policy concern since the late 1980s/early 1990s, with the creation of the Intergovernmental Panel on Climate Change (IPCC) in 1988 by the World Meteorological Organization (WMO) and the United Nations Environment Program (UNEP), and the publication of the first IPCC Assessment Report in 1990. These were followed by the development and subsequent ratification of the 1992 United Nations Framework Convention on Climate Change and the 1997 Kyoto Protocol, and the development and implementation of extensive climate change policy frameworks and regulation in many countries. As has been discussed in Chapters 4 and 5, the period 2005–2007 was a key tipping point in the debate about the roles and responsibility of the corporate sector for climate change. There was wide agreement about the importance of taking action on climate change across key stakeholder groups (politicians, the media, civil society, consumers) and most of the world's major economies. There was also a sense that regulation and policy action were inevitable, with companies (both inside and outside the European Union) pointing to the European Union Emissions Trading Scheme as evidence that governments were likely to introduce further climate change-related regulation and that this legislation would be demanding in terms of the price that would be attached to carbon and the emission reductions that would be expected of companies.

Despite these changes, and despite its very significant direct and indirect greenhouse gas emissions, relatively little specific, targeted attention was paid to the supermarket or retail sector. There are various reasons for this, reflecting the specific needs and interests of the stakeholders involved.

For NGOs, and the media, perhaps the most obvious reason was that retailers, unlike, for example, mining, oil and gas or electricity companies, were not obvious polluters. This was compounded by the lack of a 'silver-bullet solution' for reducing emissions from retailers; rather, emissions would be reduced through the cumulative contribution of a whole series of relatively small actions, implemented over extended periods of time. A further challenge was that there was no consensus about the responsibility that retailers should bear for the greenhouse gas emissions associated with the products that they sold or for the manner in which these products were subsequently used or consumed by their customers. Together, these factors made it difficult for NGOs to create compelling, media-friendly narratives about the retail sector and climate change. The consequence was that, when they did focus on the retail sector, NGOs concentrated on specific products (e.g. encouraging a shift from incandescent to more energy-efficient lightbulbs, encouraging domestic insulation) or specific aspects of consumer lifestyles (e.g. encouraging the use of public transport) rather than focusing on the retail sector's wider carbon footprint.

In most countries, buildings and transport (the sources of most of the retail sector's own emissions) were already covered by regulations, codes and standards. Specific products, in particular electrical goods, also had their energy consumption regulated. Furthermore, energy prices and wider climate change policies (e.g. carbon taxes) provided further incentives for retailers to reduce their energy consumption and greenhouse gas emissions. The consequence was that, from a regulatory perspective, it was not clear what more could be achieved by introducing regulations specifically targeted at the retail sector.

While investors had an active role in encouraging other sectors to take action on climate change, they were less active in the retail sector. One reason was that the sector's total energy costs were relatively low, typically representing 1 to 2% of corporate turnover, which meant that most investors did not see energy as an important driver of long-term business value for the sector (for a more detailed discussion of 'financial materiality', see Sullivan, 2011a). Another reason was that the sector was not seen as being at particular risk from regulation or from NGO campaigns. Most investors saw climate change primarily as a cost and efficiency issue, rather than a strategic value driver or a significant business risk. Interestingly, despite this, a number of company interviewees highlighted investors as a key stakeholder and explained that much of their reporting was focused on investor needs. They explained that, even on non-financially material issues, investors compare and rank companies and it was therefore important that they performed well relative to their peers on issues such as their carbon footprint per unit of floor area.

Finally, peer pressure played out differently in different markets. It was very important in the UK, where there was a clear competition for leadership on climate change. It was, however, less important in the US, where retailers tended to wait to see what benefits accrued to leadership companies, before looking to take action. In contrast, in Japan, peer pressure manifested itself as a tendency towards homogeneity, with retailers tending to copy each other, rather than seeking to take a leadership position.

The evidence from the retail sector also demonstrates the important role played by corporate action in determining whether external pressures for action will emerge and the intensity of these pressures. The case-studies in Chapters 4 and 5 show that, in situations where companies have taken action and built a narrative around taking action, it can be difficult for stakeholders to argue that further or different action is required. An example is provided by energy efficiency where many companies presented energy efficiency – which aligns with wider corporate motivations for efficiency and cost-saving – as a central element of their response to climate change. This narrative clearly influenced and shaped NGO dialogue with companies, with many of the most active NGOs tending to emphasise energy efficiency rather than focusing on overall corporate carbon footprints.

A related issue is that the specific disclosures provided by companies influence the emergence of stakeholder pressures. The fact that corporate disclosures make it difficult to meaningfully differentiate between companies reduces the likelihood that governance pressures will emerge because of the difficulty of holding companies to account.

What makes external governance pressures more intense (and harder to ignore)?

While the individual pressures exerted by stakeholders on the retail sector between 2000 and 2015 were relatively weak, Chapters 4 and 5 provide us with insights into the factors that make these pressures more or less likely to be effective or that increase – or decrease – the intensity of the pressures being exerted. Four factors were identified as being of particular importance.

The first is alignment. That is, in situations where external pressures reinforce or support each other, it is more likely that they will lead to companies taking action. This was seen in the UK where the step change in the sector's focus on climate change from 2006 to 2008 was not catalysed by regulation directly targeted at the sector but rather resulted from the interaction of a variety of external pressures and incentives, including market conditions, social expectations, media portrayals, customer concerns and peer pressure. Despite these external governance pressures being, individually, relatively weak, they coincided and coalesced into what were seen by companies as strong external pressure for action on climate change. Interviewees from the UK supermarkets confirmed the importance of alignment, noting that they were much more likely to feel pressure to take action in situations where different stakeholders and stakeholder groups had a common message; when these stakeholders expressed their views at the same time; and when these groups had clarity about what they expected companies to do. Interviewees also noted that the converse applies, namely that a lack of alignment is likely to weaken the intensity of the pressures being exerted and, in turn, make it less likely that companies will feel compelled to take action. The case of the US retail sector in the period 2005 to 2007 is a good example. While there was a high level of media and NGO attention on climate change and a threat that emissions trading or other economic instruments would be introduced, US retailers concluded that it was unlikely that the Federal government would introduce strong climate change legislation or allow energy prices to rise significantly. As a consequence, their climate change strategies (which mainly focused on operational energy efficiency) did not alter substantially despite the changes in the wider business context.

Even though the media is recognised as an important stakeholder, its influence is not necessarily universally positive (or negative). From 2000 to 2015, the media played an important role in raising the profile of climate change as a business issue and in communicating the facts and evidence about climate change. Most of those interviewed agreed that the quality and quantity of media coverage improved over these years. NGO interviewees acknowledged the critical role played by the media in amplifying and lending credibility to their campaign efforts. However, they also noted that the media was not always supportive of the agendas being pursued by environmental NGOs. For example, the media gave significant attention to the scientific controversies around climate change and often encouraged patterns of consumption and lifestyles that ran counter to those that might be implied by a low-carbon, low-impact world. Some company interviewees identified negative media coverage as a reason why their company had not set more ambitious climate change targets, as they were concerned that a failure to meet these targets would inevitably be interpreted as a failure, without any acknowledgement of the degree of ambition underpinning these targets.

The second factor is duration. One of the recurring themes in our interviews with companies that made strong commitments to action on climate change was that, while they may have faced relatively little direct pressure to take action on their greenhouse gas emissions, they saw these pressures as being long term in nature. For example, they were of the view that energy prices would remain high for long periods of time and that public policy action on climate change was 'inevitable'. These interviewees explained that the framing of climate change as long term and directional provided many benefits: it made it easier to justify energy efficiency and carbon reduction-related investments; it helped convince senior management that it should act on climate change; and it signalled to policymakers that companies were supportive of stable, long-term climate change policy measures. They explained that policy uncertainty (e.g. around when policy action would be taken, what measures would be adopted, and how long the policy measures would stay in place) would limit their ability to take action and their willingness to invest (see also Sullivan, 2011b; Sullivan and Blyth, 2006). This is confirmed by the Australian case-study where the lack of dependability of and confidence in public policy meant that the retailers concentrated their efforts on those areas where there was a clear financial case for action, i.e. where the benefits outweighed the costs in the absence of carbon prices or carbon taxes. The duration of external pressures is also important as it takes companies time to develop the management systems and processes they need to respond effectively and in an informed manner to the pressures being exerted on them. If external pressures are not sustained for a reasonable period – years rather than months – it is less likely that companies will develop the necessary capacities, competence, expertise, systems and processes.

While some companies, in particular those in the UK retail sector, saw the pressures to take action on climate change as likely to be a permanent feature of the policy landscape, others drew different conclusions. Some interviewees (and companies in their corporate responsibility reports) noted that a whole series of social and environmental issues – for example, organic food, food miles, climate change, energy management, responsible sourcing, recycling, ethical trading, sustainable raw materials, animal welfare – had appeared on, disappeared from and reappeared on the corporate responsibility agenda between 2000 and 2015. There were various reasons: changing campaign priorities for NGOs, changing donor and funder pressures, media and public boredom with specific issues. A number of company interviewees explained that their initial response to any new issue was simply to wait and see, as their experience had been that most issues simply disappeared from the agenda over time. This also reflected the reality in the period 2000 to 2015 that the majority of the retailers we studied actually had relatively little capacity to act on corporate responsibility issues. This led them to focus their attention on a relatively small number of issues at any time. As we see in the French case-study, once retailers had defined their priorities, it was often difficult to add new issues to the corporate responsibility agenda.

The third factor is the business case for action and how the external pressure affects costs, revenues or asset values; we discuss the business case in further detail below.

The fourth factor is the capacity and ability of stakeholders to critically analyse corporate practice and performance. Interviewees were clear that the pressure on them to take action was inevitably greater in situations where the stakeholders involved had the resources and technical skills to critically analyse actions and performance data, make meaningful comparisons between retailers and assess corporate performance against wider benchmarks of good practice. This was heightened in cases when the stakeholder or its advisors understood the company and the sector, as this knowledge meant that the stakeholder was seen as more credible. It also meant that the stakeholder was more likely to be able to clearly articulate its expectations, in terms of the actions that it expected the company to take. In many ways, consumer pressure, as discussed above, fails on all these counts; consumers do not have the ability or resources to understand or interpret corporate data nor do they have a clear understanding of what they might ask retailers to do. This is compounded by the weaknesses in corporate climate change disclosures, the business framing of climate change as an efficiency issue and the business positioning of climate change as a complex, technical issue. This positioning is deliberate as it allows companies to argue that it is companies that are best placed to define the actions that should be taken, and to argue that the views of NGOs and other stakeholders are of less relevance to these decision-making processes.

In summary, our research suggests that external governance pressures are more likely to be effective and/or be perceived as having greater intensity in situations where they are aligned, where they are of reasonable duration, when they align with (or target) business interests, and when the stakeholders involved have the capacity and expertise necessary to effectively engage with companies over extended periods of time. Conversely, external governance pressures are less likely to be effective when they are not aligned, when they are of short duration, when they do not target business interests or when the stakeholders involved do not have the capacity or expertise to engage effectively with the company.

Internal governance

External pressures, no matter how intense or long-lived, do not automatically or inevitably lead to changes in corporate practice. These pressures are mediated through internal governance conditions and it is the results of this mediation which informs the actions that are taken. The specific actions that are taken, therefore, depend not only on the characteristics of the external governance pressures but on how this pressure is interpreted or understood by the company, on the company's willingness to respond, and on the company's ability to respond. It also depends on the characteristics of the company (e.g. its products and services, its strategy, its position in the marketplace, its geographic breadth), on how these characteristics affect the impacts of external pressures on costs, brand, sales and other relevant aspects of the business, and on how important these impacts are to the business. To present a very simplified example, a retailer whose primary point of differentiation is price is likely to be highly sensitive to pressures that affect operational costs or product costs, but less likely to be sensitive to factors that affect the corporate brand.

Our research points to three factors that are of particular importance in determining the responsiveness, or lack of responsiveness, of companies to external governance pressures. These are the business case for action, management attitudes and perceptions, and management systems, processes, organisational resources and capacities.

The business case for action and inaction

Chapters 4 and 5 are unequivocal. The vast majority of the actions taken by retailers to reduce their greenhouse gas emissions (in particular, those that involved significant capital investment or significant organisational resources) were justified on the basis of the financial costs and the benefits of the actions taken. Across the companies and countries that we have studied and the interviews we have conducted, it was clear that companies rarely took actions that were not underpinned by a clear and robust business case demonstrating that the investment met the company's financial requirements. This does not mean that companies did not get other benefits from these actions (e.g. positive press coverage, better employee engagement) but these benefits were generally not considered in the formal cost-benefit assessment process that such investments needed to go through.

Another important insight from our research was that there was a striking consistency in the financial expectations that the retailers had of their investments in energy-saving and greenhouse gas emission reduction initiatives. All expected these investments to deliver relatively short payback periods (of the order of two or three years is the norm). These expectations were similar to the rates of return expected of other capital investments, suggesting that energy efficiency and greenhouse gas emission reduction-related expenditures faced similar investment hurdles to other capital investments. In practice, this meant that, unless the retailer had a dedicated pot of money allocated for energy efficiency-related investments (which some did), climate change and energy-related investments were competing for capital with other projects. This placed them at a disadvantage given that companies, in general, tended to prefer investments that enable business growth.

It is also noteworthy that the expected returns on individual investments were the same in those companies that had made strong commitments to action on climate change and those that had not. We identified two distinct approaches to target-setting – those that conducted a detailed cost-benefit assessment of the options available to them and then set targets based on what could be achieved in a cost-effective manner, and those that set targets and then challenged the organisation to achieve these. We could not find any evidence that the latter group was any less focused on financial returns. That is, the corporate targets were not seen as open-ended commitments that must be achieved at all costs but as commitments that would be delivered if there was also a robust business case for action. It could, perhaps somewhat cynically, be suggested that corporate leaders can make bold rhetorical statements or adopt ambitious targets knowing that other corporate governance structures are in place that will ensure that only measures supported by a strong business case will actually be adopted.

Interviewees noted that the specific projects that get funded and the level of capital invested in energy efficiency and carbon reduction was strongly dependent on prevailing energy prices and the assumptions that companies were making about future energy prices. This is clearly illustrated by our analysis of the UK and US retailers. The consistent message from the UK retailers was that they expected energy prices to remain high, that they saw energy prices as more likely to increase rather than decrease, and that they expected energy prices to be more volatile. They also pointed to the high likelihood that there would be climate change-related regulation that would further increase, or at least underpin, energy prices. While these assumptions did not alter their investment requirements, they did increase the number of projects that were likely to meet their investment hurdles. In contrast, US energy prices were consistently lower than those in the UK and the threat of climate change-related legislation much less. The effect was that US retailers saw the commercial case for investing in energy efficiency as a lower priority and had fewer projects that met their investment thresholds.

How perceptions of pressures change the scope

While the business case for action is the key influence on the specific capital investment decisions made by companies, external governance pressures (and perceptions of these pressures) are important influences on companies' wider responses to climate change. The exact influence, or relevance of these pressures, depends on companies' business strategies and their market position. At one extreme, for companies who see themselves primarily as being a low-cost business, those pressures that impact on costs are seen as significantly more important than those that impact on non-financial aspects of the business. For these companies (e.g. those in the German retail sector), external governance pressures that do not affect costs or financial performance are likely to have a limited effect on the decisions that they make. At the other extreme, companies that seek to position themselves as leaders on sustainability issues or that are in markets where corporate responsibility is a potential source of competitive advantage tend to assign more weight to non-financial pressures and are more likely to be responsive to these pressures. However, even for this latter group of companies, the reality is that costs remain of the highest importance and the case-studies in Chapters 4 and 5 suggest that it is relatively unusual for non-financial considerations to trump the business case for action.

Another important influence on how companies respond to external pressures are the views that they hold on climate change as a business issue and, specifically, whether they see it as an issue of strategic importance. Those that acknowledge climate change as an important issue are more likely to respond to pressures that relate to climate change, whereas those that do not acknowledge it as an important issue are less likely to respond. This is illustrated by the French retail sector, whose perception of climate change since it first appeared on the corporate agenda in the early 2000s was that it was primarily a regulatory compliance and operational cost issue, rather than a strategic value driver. There were various reasons for French retailers to draw this conclusion: energy was a relatively small part of the retailers' cost base, there was little direct pressure on the retailers to reduce their emissions, there was no overarching regulation of corporate entities, and other sustainability issues were seen as much more pressing. While the period 2006–2008 saw the French retailers pay somewhat more attention to climate change, climate change continued to be seen primarily as an operational issue. A similar picture can be seen in the US, where US retailers consistently framed climate change as primarily an issue of cost savings and business efficiency. While the period 2005–2007 was potentially a key tipping point, the fact that the US government did not take strong regulatory action at this time was seen by the retailers as confirmation of their view that climate change was an issue of operational rather than strategic importance.

In the UK, the industry's social licence to operate was an important influence on the retail sector's response to climate change, encouraging it to move beyond a focus on energy efficiency in buildings and in transport. In the early to mid-2000s, the sector was criticised because of its impacts on local economies and specific business practices (e.g. the downward pressure on prices paid to farmers and other suppliers). The sector's actions on climate change, in particular its efforts to improve the environmental and energy performance of its suppliers, were part of the sector's broader efforts to protect its social licence to operate and reduce the risk of further regulation.

Systems, processes, resources and capacities

By 2015, almost all of the retailers covered in Chapters 4 and 5 had developed the basic management systems and processes they needed to respond to climate change. These systems and processes generally included defined responsibilities within the organisation (including board or senior management responsibility for those that saw climate change as a strategic value driver), a climate change policy setting out the organisation's views on the risks and opportunities presented by climate change, a greenhouse gas emission inventory, targets for greenhouse gas emission reductions and energy efficiency, and some reporting on climate change practices and performance.

These systems were developed at different times. Some retailers developed these prior to 2005, as part of their processes for managing their wider sustainability and corporate responsibility efforts. Others developed them more recently, with many having at least the basic management infrastructure in place by 2008 or 2009 (i.e. shortly after what we have identified as the climate change tipping point in the period 2005–2007). Many of those with pre-existing systems strengthened them at this time, through making climate change an issue of board-level importance, strengthening their targets and allocating significant resources to energy efficiency and greenhouse gas emission reductions. In interviews, companies explained that the external governance pressures they faced had driven these changes. Even those that continued to see climate change as an operational issue acknowledged that they needed to be prepared in case the external pressures strengthened and they faced greater pressure to take action. These findings reinforce the importance of ensuring that external governance pressures are sustained for reasonable periods of time. The evidence from the case-studies suggests that these pressures needed to be sustained for a number of years in order for companies to develop their internal governance systems and processes and, critically, to shift management views on the strategic importance of climate change. The case-studies also suggest that if external pressures are not sustained or are not seen as long-term features of the business landscape, companies will not move from the view that climate change is primarily an operational issue.

Even though companies strengthened their management systems and processes, their responses to climate change (i.e. the actions taken) varied. Some, for example the UK retailers, adopted stronger targets and intensified their efforts to reduce their greenhouse gas emissions. Others continued to focus attention on improving operational energy efficiency. That is, the adoption of more formal management systems did not necessarily change management views, nor did it necessarily result in significant changes in the actions being taken or the resources being committed to action on climate change. What these systems did do was to enable companies to position themselves to respond more effectively to external governance pressures, through enabling them to identify emerging issues and respond in a timely, effective manner.

This is a disappointing conclusion as it suggests that management systems offer relatively little in terms of changing corporate practice. However, much more encouraging conclusions emerge when we analyse these systems as iterative processes, i.e. when we look at how experiences with the implementation of emission reduction initiatives and, in particular, targets, affect these organisations. Many of the interviewees noted that their past experiences with action on environmental and energy issues were a critical determinant of their willingness to do more on these issues. Those companies that had been able to extract cost savings or other business benefits through focusing on energy use or greenhouse gas emissions were more open to taking further action on these issues. For example, interviewees from the UK supermarket sector were clear that the success of their efforts to reduce their own greenhouse gas emissions had given them the confidence to invest effort in reducing emissions from their supply chains. They also commented that these successes meant that their senior managers were supportive of further efforts to reduce emissions and were more open to the idea that the company should engage with its customers and suppliers on these issues. While we did not identify this in our research, we acknowledge that the converse also applies. A lack of initial success in saving costs may undermine a company's willingness to take further action, and may also makes the organisation as a whole, and individuals within the organisation, reluctant to develop their skills or to invest effort in understanding the importance of these issues to the business.

One of the key themes that emerged from our interviews was that formal systems and processes for managing greenhouse gas emissions and energy use enable organisations to respond effectively to external pressures and to deliver on their own corporate policies. Within this, the setting of targets – and the associated processes of assigning responsibilities for the delivery of these targets, the allocation of financial and other resources for the delivery of these targets, the monitoring of performance against these targets, internal and external reporting – was highlighted by many of the interviewees. Targets are important because of their direct role in translating corporate policies into tangible action. Longer-term targets also allow climate change and energy efficiency-related investments to be better aligned with business investment cycles. This is well illustrated by the manner on which the UK supermarkets used their target-setting processes to ensure that cost-effective innovations were deployed across the entire business; most had targets relating to the development of green stores, the testing of green technologies, and the wider deployment of cost-effective technologies and approaches across their business, and also had requirements that new technologies were integrated into store refurbishment and upgrade processes. The delivery of these targets led to them developing significant competence and knowledge in energy management, and gave them a long pipeline of improvements that they could roll out across their building estates and transport fleets.

Concluding comments: designing effective governance interventions

This book provides us with clear insights into how stakeholders can design and deploy governance interventions (or create pressure) that encourage companies to take effective action on climate change (or other corporate responsibility issues). It also tells us much about the factors that stakeholders need to consider or be aware of when deciding on what they might do to encourage companies to change their practices and processes.

The reality is that companies create narratives and frameworks that support their view of the world and the way in which they wish to engage with the world. On occasion, these will align with a stakeholder's views, in which case the company is more likely to respond constructively to that stakeholder. It is also essential to recognise that the business case for action defines the actions that companies will take. Of course, stakeholders can argue that companies should take a longer-term view or that they should be prepared to accept lower returns on investments that provide clear social or environmental benefits. However, such arguments are unlikely to carry much sway with corporate decision-makers. Stakeholders may have more influence if they can challenge companies on some of the underlying assumptions that they are making (e.g. on future energy prices, the likelihood of regulation, the business case for action, the risks of inaction).

If you are designing and deploying governance interventions (or looking to influence companies), we offer the following six guiding recommendations:

1   You are more likely to be effective when the issues you are concerned about are also of concern to other stakeholders. Alignment is key to maximise your influence and likelihood of success.
2   You need to be consistent, and commit to campaigning over years not months. Companies often assume – with good reason – that external

pressures will dwindle or disappear over time and, therefore, 'wait and see' is a common response to external pressures.

3 You need to understand the commercial, competitive and other dynamics of the sector and of the individual companies you are focusing on. Is the market one where competitive differentiation is a driver of corporate behaviour (and therefore strategies like benchmarking may be effective), or is it one where collective engagement is needed in order to drive change? Does the company aspire to be a leader on corporate responsibility, or does it compete primarily on the basis of cost or quality?

4 You need to be clear about the changes you want to deliver and the outcomes you want to achieve. For example, are you interested in improving business efficiency or in delivering absolute improvements in performance or impact? You also need to be clear how these changes are to be delivered – what are the specific actions that you expect companies to take?

5 You need to understand the data that are available (what it means, how companies compare to each other, how companies compare to your expectations). This takes work and a willingness to interrogate and properly analyse the information that companies and others provide.

6 You need to focus on companies' objectives and targets. Objectives and targets are the engine that drive corporate action, that ensure that action is taken and appropriate resources are allocated. They also drive the development of capacity and expertise, ensuring that companies continue to improve over time.

7 The implications for climate change

In Chapter 6, we discussed how our research has contributed to our understanding of the relationships and interactions between external governance pressures, internal governance conditions and corporate responses (or actions). In this chapter we analyse what this research tells us about the potential for governance pressures and processes to influence corporate practice and performance on climate change. We pay particular attention to the outcomes achieved to date, and how these compare to the outcomes that are required if we are to prevent the most serious impacts of climate change. We also discuss the outcomes that might be achieved if external governance pressures and/or internal governance processes were strengthened, if actors such as investors and NGOs made greater use of existing governance frameworks and mechanisms, and if governments were to adopt more interventionist approaches to regulation.

What corporate greenhouse gas emissions reductions are needed to avoid dangerous climate change? Framing the discussion

Chapters 4 and 5 provided us with insights into the performance of companies relative to each other and into the performance of groups of companies in one country relative to those in other countries. We now extend this analysis to consider how these performance outcomes achieved compared to the performance outcomes we might need to achieve if we are to avert dangerous climate change. We divide this analysis into two parts. First, we consider companies' performance in the context of the policies and expectations that existed in 2015, i.e. at the end of the period covered by our research. We then update this reference framework to consider both global trends in emissions and global policy developments in the subsequent five-year period, i.e. through to the beginning of 2020.

Framing the discussion: policy expectations in 2015

In its Fifth Assessment Report, the Intergovernmental Panel on Climate Change (IPCC) used a set of four scenarios (which it referred to as Representative Concentration Pathways or RCPs) to model the effects of future greenhouse gas emissions (IPCC, 2014a, 2014b). The IPCC stated that reaching atmospheric concentration levels of 430 to 530 ppm CO_2e by 2100 (broadly considered as the range required to keep the global average temperature rise below 2°C) would require significant cuts in greenhouse gas emissions in both the medium and long term. It noted that the majority of scenarios that envisaged reaching 430 to 480 ppm CO_2e by 2100 were associated with greenhouse gas emission reductions of between 40 and 70% by 2050 compared to 2010. For scenarios that limited atmospheric greenhouse gas concentrations to between 480 and 530 ppm CO_2e in 2100 and did not exceed this concentration at any point during the century, the IPCC suggested that global greenhouse gas emissions would need to be reduced by between 40 and 55% by 2050 compared to 2010. These equate to reductions in absolute global greenhouse gas emissions of between 1.26% (for a 40% reduction) and 2.96% (for a 70% reduction) per annum over the period 2010 to 2050.

Even though the IPCC itself did not offer a view on the greenhouse gas emission reductions that should be achieved by individual countries, it was generally recognised that the need for economic growth and increased access to energy in low-income countries would result in increased greenhouse gas emissions from these countries in the near term. This, in turn, suggested that high-income countries would need to bear a greater burden of the emission reduction effort. So how did national policy targets in 2015 compare to these global targets? The high-level commitments that had been made by the European Union (EU) and by Australia, France, Germany, Japan, the United Kingdom and the United States (the six countries covered by our research) are presented in Table 7.1. These commitments broadly translated into annual, economy-wide greenhouse gas emission reductions of between 1 and 1.5% per annum through to 2020 and, in the case of the EU and the UK's 2050 targets, over 2.5% per annum over the period 1990 to 2050. These emission reduction commitments, at least through to 2020 or 2025, fell well short of those suggested by the IPCC, suggesting ether that these countries intended to significantly accelerate their efforts after 2020 or that they would not be able to reduce their emissions in line with the reductions needed to keep the global temperature rise below 2°C (see, further, Boyd, Cranston-Turner and Ward, 2015; Boyd, Stern and Ward, 2015; Jeffery et al., 2015; Stern and Taylor, 2010).

Another way of analysing the greenhouse gas emission reductions required was provided by consultants PWC in its annual Low Carbon Economy Index which analysed the rate of decarbonisation (measured in terms of greenhouse gas emissions per unit of GDP) of the global economy compared to the rate needed to limit global warming to 2°C. In its 2014 report, PWC estimated that the global economy needed to decarbonise at a rate of 6.2% a year, more than five times faster than the rate achieved in 2013 (PWC, 2014).

Framing the discussion: policy expectations in 2020

In 2018, the IPCC issued a special report on the impacts of global warming of 1.5°C above pre-industrial levels and related global greenhouse gas emission

Table 7.1 National greenhouse gas emission reduction targets (in 2015)

Country/region	Proposed targets	Annual equivalent reduction (%)	Source
EU	Achieve at least a 20% reduction in greenhouse gas emissions by 2020 compared to 1990.	0.74	European Union (2009)
	Reduce greenhouse gas emissions by 30% by 2020 compared to 1990, subject to other developed countries committing themselves to comparable emission reductions and economically more advanced developing countries committing themselves to contributing adequately according to their responsibilities and capabilities.	1.18	European Union (2009)
	Reduce greenhouse gas emissions by at least 40% by 2030 compared to 1990.	1.27	European Commission (2014)
	Reduce greenhouse gas emissions by at least 80% by 2050, against a 1990 baseline, or by 80–95% as part of efforts by developed countries as a group to reduce their emissions by a similar degree.	2.65–4.87	European Commission (2011)
United Kingdom	Reduce greenhouse gas emissions by at least 34% by 2020, against a 1990 baseline.	1.37	Department of Energy and Climate Change (2012)
	Reduce greenhouse gas emissions by 16% by 2020, against a 2005 baseline.	1.15	European Union (2009)
	Reduce greenhouse gas emissions by at least 80% by 2050, against a 1990 baseline.	2.65	Department of Energy and Climate Change (2012)
France	Reduce greenhouse gas emissions by 14% by 2020, against a 2005 baseline.	1.00	European Union (2009)

(continued)

Table 7.1 (continued)

Country/region	Proposed targets	Annual equivalent reduction (%)		Source
Germany	Reduce greenhouse gas emissions by 14% by 2020, against a 2005 baseline.	1.00		European Union (2009)
United States	Reduce greenhouse gas emissions by 17% by 2020 against a 2005 baseline.	1.23		US Climate Action Network (2014)
	Reduce greenhouse gas emissions by 26–28% by 2025 against a 2005 baseline and make best efforts to reduce emissions by 28%.		1.49–1.63	US White House (2014)
Japan	Reduce greenhouse gas emissions by 25% by 2020 against a 1990 baseline.	0.95		US Climate Action Network (2014)
Australia	Reduce greenhouse gas emissions by between 5 and 25% (depending on actions by other countries) by 2020 against a 2000 baseline.		0.26–1.43	US Climate Action Network (2014)

pathways (IPCC, 2018). The report's key finding was that meeting a 1.5°C target was possible but would require deep emission reductions and rapid, far-reaching and unprecedented changes in all aspects of society. It cautioned that even assuming full implementation of the commitments (the Nationally Determined Contributions) made by signatories to the Paris Agreement would see net global greenhouse emissions increase compared to 2010, leading to a warming of about 3°C by 2100, and more thereafter (see, also, UNEP, 2019). The report suggested that, for global warming to be limited to 1.5°C, global net human-caused emissions of carbon dioxide (CO_2) would need to fall by about 45% from 2010 levels by 2030 (a rate of approximately 4.1% per annum), and reach net zero around 2050. In its 2019 annual Emissions Gap Report, the UN Environment Programme (UNEP) stated that global greenhouse gas emissions needed to fall by 7.6% each year between 2020 and 2030 in order for the 1.5°C temperature goal to be met (UNEP, 2019).

These conclusions on the level of emission reductions required were echoed by PWC in the 2019 iteration of its annual Low Carbon Economy Index (PWC, 2019). It stated that the carbon intensity of the global economy fell by 1.6% in 2018, less than half of the decarbonisation rate of 3.3% seen in 2015. PWC estimated a decarbonisation rate of 7.5% per year would be required to give a two-thirds probability of limiting warming to 2°C, while a rate of 11.3% would be needed to keep warming to 1.5°C.

There were signs of a renewed policy focus on climate change in 2019. Ten countries, including the UK, France, Canada and Ireland, declared a 'climate emergency'. The UK became the first major economy to legislate a net-zero emissions target, with other countries – including Sweden, Costa Rica, Denmark, France, Germany and New Zealand – all stating that they intended to achieve net-zero emissions (or equivalent) by 2050. However, the picture was not unambiguously positive; the United States stated that it was formally withdrawing from the Paris Agreement on Climate Change and, despite the commitments made by other governments, none of the world's largest greenhouse gas emitters – China, the United States and India – made any zero-carbon commitments at the national level (although many US states did make such commitments).

How do corporate emission reductions compare to those required to avoid dangerous climate change?

Some caution is required when deciding what emission reductions should be expected of companies. While the various emission reductions targets outlined above provide a broad frame of reference for assessing the effectiveness of corporate action on climate change, there may not be a direct correspondence between these targets and the emission reductions achieved by companies. For example, governments may decide that different sectors of the economy should have different emission reduction targets, governments may focus their efforts on specific sectors (e.g. electricity generation) where the benefits cascade through to other sectors, or there may be disagreement on the scope of companies' responsibilities and influence (e.g. whether companies should be accountable for their operation emissions or for their wider carbon footprint, whether companies should focus on areas where they have influence – e.g. customer education, public policy lobbying – or where they have control).

While we acknowledge these limitations, we see that the different emission reduction targets and commitments above provide a useful range of expectations that we can use to assess corporate climate change performance, both historic (i.e. in terms of the actual emission reductions achieved) and expected future emissions performance (as set out in corporate objectives and targets).

Historic emission reductions: impressive and consistent but not ambitious enough

From the data presented in Chapters 4 and 5, all of the global retailers consistently improved their energy efficiency between 2000 and 2015. This reflects the general trend in most advanced economies for reasonably consistent improvements in energy efficiency (as measured in terms of energy used per unit of economic output). Examples of the improvements achieved include:

- UK retailers achieved annual average improvements in their greenhouse gas emissions and energy intensity of approximately 4% per annum over the period 2007 to 2012.
- Woolworths' greenhouse gas emissions per unit of turnover declined by 14% over the period 2009 to 2013.
- In Germany, Metro reduced its energy consumption per square metre of selling space by between 2 and 3% per annum over the period 2001 to 2013, and REWE reduced its greenhouse gas emissions per unit of floor area by 31.8% over the period 2006 to 2012.
- The US retailers CVS Caremark and Walmart reduced their energy and/or emissions intensity by approximately 3% per annum over the period 2007 to 2013.
- In France, Auchan reduced its average electricity consumption per unit of shop floor area in its hypermarkets by approximately 3.5% per annum from 2009 to 2013, while Carrefour reduced its energy consumption per square metre of sales area by approximately 3.3% per annum from 2004 to 2013.

Despite these improvements, business growth and changes in business models have exerted a strong upward pressure on absolute greenhouse gas emissions and total energy consumption. For example, in the UK, despite the 4% per annum improvements in greenhouse gas emissions intensity between 2007 and 2012, while four companies reduced their absolute greenhouse gas emissions, three saw their emissions increase. Across the seven UK supermarkets, average absolute emissions only declined by approximately 1.1% per year over this period. A similar picture is seen in the United States. For the eight US companies where at least three years' data were available, five succeeded in reducing their absolute greenhouse gas emissions, three saw their emissions increase and they averaged a 0.6% per annum reduction in their greenhouse gas emissions. A similar picture can be seen in the other geographies studied; all of the companies improved their emissions and energy intensity but only some succeeded in delivering absolute reductions in greenhouse gas emissions.

A recurring theme from our interviews with retailers was that while it is feasible to reduce absolute greenhouse gas emissions for a number of years in succession, it is difficult to sustain these reductions over extended periods of time. There are different factors at play. Most obviously, business growth – in terms of the number of stores and in terms of sales floor area – can exert upward pressure on emissions. In the period 2000 to 2015, changes in consumer demand (e.g. the growth in demand for fresh produce) and consumer habits (e.g. the growth in online shopping) also increased energy demand and greenhouse gas emissions. Of course, this argument about the tension between business growth and total emissions must be qualified by noting that the historic evolution of the sector may not be a good guide to the future. However, the fact that many of the retailers had – and continue to have – target business growth rates of 3 to 5% per annum makes the challenge clear; companies need to consistently deliver significant improvements in their emissions and energy intensity simply to keep their absolute emissions reasonably stable, let alone deliver the sort of emission reductions suggested by national governments or by the IPCC. Put another way, they are effectively running to stand still.

Objectives and targets: more ambitious but still not enough

In western multinationals, the setting of objectives and targets is usually the point where corporate policies are translated into concrete action. By 2014 or 2015, many of the world's largest retailers had set targets for their operations and other activities under their direct control. For example:

- Seven & i's targets included reducing electricity consumption per unit of floor area per hour in its Seven-Eleven stores in Japan by 1% per annum and reducing the total Scope 1 and Scope 2 CO_2 emissions per unit of floor area per hour in its Ito-Yokado stores by 1% per annum.
- Aeon's objective was to reduce its emissions per unit of floor area by 50% from 2010 to 2020.
- Metro had a goal of reducing its greenhouse gas emissions per square metre of selling area by 20% by 2020 compared to a 2011 baseline.
- REWE Group aimed to halve its greenhouse gas emissions per unit of retail floor area by 2022 against a baseline of 2006.
- CVS Caremark had a target of reducing its total Scope 1 and Scope 2 emissions per unit of floor area by 15% over the period 2010 to 2018.
- Lowe's set a target of reducing its greenhouse gas emissions per unit of floor area by 20% over the period 2010 to 2020.
- Carrefour had target of reducing its electricity consumption per square metre of sales floor area by 30% over the period 2004 to 2020.

While virtually all of the retailers covered by our research expected their emissions and/or energy intensity to improve over time, there was a notable divergence in relation to the question of whether absolute emissions would increase or decrease. A number of UK supermarkets had set targets to reduce their absolute emissions by more than 1.5% per annum, with some of these targets running for ten years or more. In addition, in Australia, Coles was targeting absolute reductions in greenhouse gas emissions of 3–4% per year, against a backdrop of ongoing business growth, and Woolworths had a commitment to stabilise its facility-related greenhouse gas emissions at 2007 levels by 2015. In contrast, most of the other retailers had not set targets for their absolute greenhouse gas emissions or had signalled that they expected their emissions to grow over time. For example, Seven & i stated that it saw the expansion and development of new stores and new products as inevitable, even though this was likely to lead to increases in electricity consumption. Similarly, Metro stated that it expected its absolute Scope 1 and 2 emissions to increase by 18% over the period 2006 to 2015 because of its business expansion, and CVS Caremark, Home Depot Inc, Lowe's and Target all expected their absolute emissions to increase as their businesses grew. In aggregate, the emissions growth trajectories predicted by many of the retailers were in direct conflict with the targets being set by governments (which envisaged absolute economy-wide greenhouse gas emission reductions of between 1 and 1.5% per annum through to 2020) and the predictions from the IPCC which suggested that reductions of between 2.5% and 4% per annum were required over the period 2010 to 2050.

These somewhat depressing conclusions should be qualified by acknowledging that a few retailers had made commitments to reducing the emissions associated with their supply chains and customers, that some – notably in the UK – had made emission reduction commitments that aligned with the targets being set by governments, and that almost all were looking to significantly improve their energy efficiency. While, in total, these may fall short of the reductions suggested by the IPCC, they also, if achieved, represent a potentially significant contribution to society's overall greenhouse gas reduction efforts.

A critical question in this context is whether these commitments are plausible, i.e. is it likely that they can, all things being equal, be delivered by companies? Plausibility can be assessed by looking at the level of detail underpinning targets (where the greater the detail, the greater likelihood that the company understands how it intends to achieve its targets), the company's history in meeting previous commitments (where a high level of target delivery should provide a greater degree of confidence that current targets will be met), and historic performance (where an alignment or consistency with historic emissions performance should provide a higher degree of confidence) (adapted from Sullivan and Gouldson, 2013). In relation to the level of detail underpinning targets, most of the retailers that had set emission reduction targets between 2000 and 2015 had also published supplementary targets that underpinned these overarching commitments. They also described the main actions that they intended to take to deliver their commitments, the emission reductions or energy savings that they expected to result from these actions, and the financial resources that they had allocated to the delivery of these commitments. That is, most of the retailers had reasonably clear strategies for the delivery of their climate change commitments. They also had a good track record of delivering on historic climate change targets. Of perhaps equal importance for their credibility was the fact that they usually provided explanations in situations where targets have not been met. Finally, most of the targets that were in place in 2014 and 2015 were broadly similar to the performance outcomes that had been achieved in the preceding decade. To take just one example, UK supermarkets, historically, improved their emissions or energy intensity by between 3 and 5% per annum and, in aggregate, this had enabled the sector to deliver approximately a 1% per annum reduction in its total greenhouse gas emissions. In this context, the absolute performance being targeted by the UK retailers in 2014 and 2015 – which, for those that had set absolute targets, equated to a 1.5% per annum reduction in absolute greenhouse gas emissions– was broadly consistent with the longer-term performance of the sector. Taken together, these different frames of analysis suggest that the retailers were capable of delivering on the commitments that they have made.

Another important policy question relates to the longevity of corporate commitments to action on climate change. Many corporations have been happy enough to take voluntary action and to sustain this commitment for a number of years because there are often economic returns from doing so (Gouldson and Sullivan, 2013). The question is what happens once the easy options have been exploited? Do companies learn from the early phases of transition so that, when the challenges become more significant, they are better able to cope? Or will they continue to take action so long as it is economically attractive to do so, but then gradually withdraw their active support and drift towards active opposition as the changes required become more challenging? One of the central findings from our discussions with company representatives was the confidence that they had in their efficiency-related targets. They noted that their trialling of new technologies combined with their management processes (e.g. targets relating to the development of green stores, targets relating to the deployment of innovative technologies and approaches across their business) meant that they had a high degree of visibility – with five or seven years not being uncommon – on the rate of adoption of these new technologies and the emission reductions or energy savings that they could expect to achieve.

Of course, it is by no means a given that companies will set progressively more demanding targets or that, once they have set absolute emission reduction targets, they will continue to do so. In our research, we identified examples of companies making commitments but not reporting on performance against these commitments. For example, in 2008, Aeon committed to reducing its greenhouse gas emissions by 30% by 2012 against a 2006 baseline, and extended this in 2011 to reduce emissions from its Japanese business in 2013 against a

2006 baseline. While Aeon reported on total emissions and on emissions per unit area in its 2012 sustainability report, it only reported on emissions per unit area in its 2013 report, suggesting that its absolute target was no longer relevant to the business. We also identified cases of companies setting weaker targets than they had previously set. For example, while Auchan set a target in 2011 of reducing electricity consumption in its stores and shopping centres by 2% in 2012, it did not set a follow-up target in its 2013 sustainability report. Finally, we identified cases of companies setting targets with narrowly defined scopes. This is illustrated by Metro, which set a goal of reducing its greenhouse gas emissions per square metre of selling area by 20% by 2020 compared to a 2011 baseline. This target had a much narrower scope than Metro's previous targets, which had included logistics-related emissions. Metro justified this decision by arguing that emissions from logistics were increasing at a disproportionate rate due to its expansion into countries such as China and Russia.

Practices and processes: improved but not transformed

Analysing historic and future carbon footprints is one way of analysing whether companies or the retail sector as a whole are responding to the challenge of climate change. While this approach has the attraction of enabling a quantitative assessment to be made, it risks obscuring some of the important elements of practice – e.g. innovation, capacity-building – that are essential to making climate change a core element of corporate strategy, and to ensuring that companies play their role in enabling society as a whole to respond to climate change.

Across the 6 countries and 30 companies covered by our research, by 2015 the majority of the retailers had established the basic management infrastructure (policies, targets, accountabilities, financial and human resources) to manage climate change-related risks and opportunities in their operations. While there were variations in the details, almost all had assessed the risks and opportunities presented by climate change to their businesses, appointed staff with responsibilities for climate change and energy management, set objectives and targets, allocated resources for the delivery of these objectives and targets, established management systems and processes, and monitored and reported on performance. It was clear from our interviews that many of the retailers saw climate change and energy as areas where they wanted to continuously improve performance, and they were using their target-setting processes to drive these improvements. In addition, many of the interviewees commented that these management systems and processes had enabled their company to identify opportunities to reduce their greenhouse gas emissions or improve energy efficiency, to gather and collate the information necessary to report to their stakeholders, and to identify opportunities for new products and services.

There was also evidence that retailers would look beyond energy efficiency when trying to reduce their carbon footprint. For example, many had experimented with renewable energy, both in their stores (e.g. solar, wind, geothermal) and in transport (e.g. biofuels), with some committing to sourcing some or even all of their grid-sourced electricity from renewable sources. Despite the significant amounts of capital that had been invested in renewable energy, all were clear that they would only make investments in situations where the economics of these investments are commercially attractive. As we have noted in Chapters 4, 5 and 6, this emphasis on the need for a robust business case was a consistent theme across all of the retailers; all investments, not just those relating to renewable energy, energy efficiency and climate change, were expected to deliver payback periods of three years or less, and were expected to compete with other areas of the business for access to capital.

There were many examples of retailers engaging with their customers on climate change; examples included providing advice and guidance on environmentally responsible behaviour (e.g. encouraging lower temperature washing, replacing lightbulbs, unplugging phone chargers, keeping fridges and freezers running more efficiently, switching to showers rather than baths, encouraging home insulation), and incentivising the purchase of products such as low-energy lightbulbs. While retailers were willing to offer higher energy efficiency and 'greener' products, they were reluctant – unless compelled to do so by legislation – to remove products considered to be unsustainable.

There was also progress on product labelling, with some retailers labelling products based on how they had been transported or on the emissions embedded in the product. However, with the notable exception of energy efficiency labelling on electrical products (where the labels are widely recognised, underpinned by common standards and overseen by regulatory bodies), there was limited uptake of carbon footprinting. Various reasons were provided by interviewees: the cost of conducting the assessments, the costs of the labelling process, uncertainty around whether customers would actually use the information provided, the complexity of labelling, the potential that labels would need to be revised if there are any changes in the supply chain, the risk of over-simplification (e.g. it is not clear how to trade off different environmental variables in a single label) and the lack of consistency around reporting.

One of the most interesting – and important – areas of focus related to supply chain management. While the UK retailers had established programmes to help their agricultural suppliers reduce greenhouse gas emissions, retailers in other countries appeared to have paid much less attention to their suppliers. For example, when US retailers engaged with suppliers, the primary focus was on those aspects that directly affected the retailer (e.g. product packaging which has implications for transport), rather than on aspects such as production processes or supplier energy management. Beyond the UK, most retailers viewed climate change primarily as a problem for suppliers, with the assumption being that if climate change affected input costs, suppliers would address this problem themselves. The retailers took the view that they could manage this issue through supplier diversification and competition which would encourage suppliers to keep their costs low, either through making their operations more efficient or through absorbing some of these costs in the form of reduced profits.

Closing reflections on climate change practice and performance

Our overall assessment of the retail sector is that, by 2015, the majority of the largest companies in the sector had robust processes for managing their operational (i.e. building and transport-related) impacts, and for improving their energy efficiency and greenhouse gas emissions intensity over time. However, beyond their own operations – with notable exceptions such as those retailers that had made commitments to large-scale purchases of renewable energy or those that had structured engagement programmes with their suppliers – it is not clear that the sector as a whole had a clear and aspirational vision of what it meant to be a 'sustainable sector' or of the relationship between sustainability and sustainable consumption and business value. This was illustrated in many ways: the emphasis on energy prices and the financial case as the primary driver of corporate action, the emphasis on efficiency rather than absolute emissions, the focus on operations rather than the wider carbon footprint, the lack of alignment between corporate targets and the emission reductions suggested by the IPCC and the lack of discussion about sustainable consumption and about whether climate change would require retailers to shrink rather than grow their businesses.

However, another reading of the evidence provides grounds for a more optimistic conclusion. Some of the retailers had set targets that went well beyond those specified in government policy. While these did not go as far as the sort of reductions suggested by the IPCC, they did suggest that it is possible to create the conditions for companies to take strong, meaningful action beyond that required by law. It is also possible to look at some of the actions taken – e.g. voluntary carbon labelling, proactive public policy engagement, supplier engagement, product choice editing, supply chain targets – to see that companies can be induced to take at least some radical actions. Indeed, when one looks at the major changes in the retail sector over the past decade (e.g. the growth of internet shopping, longer opening hours, increasingly complex supply chains), it could be concluded that the retail sector has an almost unlimited capacity to adapt and change. That is, this is a sector that, with the right incentives, could play a much more proactive response in society's response to climate change. The question we now turn to is whether and how governance processes may be designed, implemented and harnessed to deliver stronger outcomes.

What can be delivered through governance processes?

External climate governance pressures differ between countries and over time

In very broad terms, we can identify four distinct combinations of external governance conditions. The first is the situation where there is limited financial pressure for action (i.e. energy prices and carbon prices are low), and where the other pressures on companies to act on climate change are weak. The second is where there is a strong financial case for action (i.e. energy prices and/or carbon prices are high), but where the other pressures on companies to act on climate change are weak. The third is where there is a weak financial case for action (i.e. energy prices and carbon prices are low), but where the pressures on companies to act on climate change are strong. Finally, the fourth is where there is a strong financial case for action (i.e. energy prices and/or carbon prices are high), and where the other pressures on companies to act on climate change are also strong.

While acknowledging that the interpretation of strength and weakness will depend on the specific company, the wider business context and internal governance conditions, our research allows two high-level predictions to be made about the corporate actions that are likely to result. The first is that the stronger the financial case, the more likely it is that companies will take action to reduce their energy consumption and/or their greenhouse gas emissions. The reason is the higher that energy prices and/or carbon prices are, the larger the number of financially attractive investment opportunities that will be available to companies. This was a clear message from all of the companies and jurisdictions studied; it was clear that reducing financial costs was the primary motivation for taking action, that those investments that offered the most attractive returns would be prioritised, and that all energy and climate-related investment needed to deliver payback periods of two or at most three years. While this is a central conclusion, this does not mean that there is a direct relationship between higher energy and carbon prices and the efforts companies will take to reduce energy consumption or greenhouse gas emissions. Companies will not respond immediately to higher prices. They need to be sure that these prices will prevail for sufficient time for them to invest and to realise a return on that investment. We saw this in Japan where, following the Great East Earthquake, reducing energy consumption was a national priority, and the retailers responded by changing operational practices (e.g. switching off equipment) and investing in more efficient equipment (e.g. LEDs). However, these pressures were not sustained and, after 12–18 months, company energy use started to rise again. Companies may also respond in other ways, e.g. they may press governments to reduce or eliminate some of the costs introduced by climate change-related legislation.

The second is that the stronger (or more aligned) the external pressures on companies, the more likely companies are take action to understand the risks and opportunities presented by climate change to their business, the more likely they are to formalise their management systems and processes, the more likely they are to set climate change-related objectives and targets, and the more likely they are to look at how they can support others (e.g. governments, suppliers, customers) to reduce their greenhouse gas emissions. However, as we have previously discussed, even in situations where there are strong external pressures on companies to take action, these actions will inevitably be constrained by the financial case. That is, the specific actions that are taken, in particular those that require capital investment, will need to be underpinned by a robust financial business case for action,

When we look at the empirical evidence from the retail sector from the late 1990s through to 2015, we see examples of each of these external governance conditions across the six countries studied. In all six countries there were significant, albeit not necessarily linear, increases in energy prices over this time-frame. In the case of Europe, these increases were compounded by the introduction of the European Union Emissions Trading Scheme in 2005 with the CO_2 allowance price reaching almost €30 per tonne in early 2006, albeit then declining to almost zero in 2007 (at the end of the Scheme's first allocation period), recovering to €25–30 per tonne in 2008 and falling to approximately €5 per tonne thereafter. In addition, the retail sector was exposed to a variety of other, non-financial, external pressures including extensive public and media attention focused on climate change, in particular in 2006 and 2007, regulation and NGO campaigns on climate change.

The different countries saw these financial and other pressures evolve in different ways. The US can be characterised as a country where the financial and the other pressures for action were consistently weak throughout the period covered by our research. As discussed in Chapter 5, US gas and electricity prices from 2005 to 2015 were typically one-half to two-thirds of those in the UK; US retailers, even in the period 2005 to 2007, considered it unlikely that the Federal government would take strong action on climate change, and there was relatively little pressure from customers or NGOs for retailers to reduce their emissions. France, Germany and Japan, in contrast, were countries where there was a consistently strong financial case for action, driven by relatively high energy prices, but where the other external pressures to act on climate change were relatively weak. The reasons differed between the three countries. In the case of Japan, it was because climate change was not a major issue for Japanese consumers, and because Japanese NGOs were relatively weak and lacked the influence and capacity to hold companies to account. In Germany and France, while the pressures for action were stronger, with significant media and NGO attention focused on climate change, these pressures were not sufficiently strong to overcome the emphasis on price as the primary point of differentiation in the German market or the competition from other sustainability issues in the case of France. Australia oscillated between weak and stronger external pressures for action, against a backdrop of rising energy prices, albeit from a very low starting point. Australian retailers acknowledged that they need to make decisions that enabled them to be successful under two distinct scenarios – one where there was strong regulatory, financial and societal pressure for action, and one where there was weak regulatory, financial and societal pressure for action – but where both scenarios were seen as equally likely. Finally, the UK can be described as a country where there was a strong financial case for action, and where the other external pressures on companies to act on climate change were also strong. In relation to the financial case for action, UK energy prices mirrored those elsewhere in Europe, with the European Union Emissions Trading Scheme exerting further upward pressure on electricity prices. In relation to external pressures, UK NGOs actively campaigned on climate change, climate change was consistently identified as an issue of consumer concern and there was strong competition amongst the UK supermarkets for the leadership position on climate change.

Internal climate governance processes have strengthened since 2000

When analysing the effect of external governance pressures on companies, it is important to acknowledge – as discussed above – that, by 2015, the majority of the retailers had reasonably well-developed climate change or energy management systems and processes. This was a significant change from the late 1990s/ early 2000s when climate change was just starting to appear as a subject of management interest, and energy management was seen as a relatively low management priority. When climate change and energy-related pressures first started to emerge in the early 2000s, most of the retailers were relatively poorly prepared to respond, and needed time to develop a proper understanding of their energy consumption and greenhouse gas emissions before they could make decisions on issues such as longer-term energy and emission-related targets. This helps to explain why the retailers started by focusing their initial attention on operational efficiency and on short-term process-related targets. As later waves of pressures hit the sector, the benefits of these systems and processes were clear. The retailers had data on energy use and emissions that had the ability to set targets and implement effective responses, and were able to effectively and credibly communicate their actions and perceptions of climate change to relevant stakeholders.

One of the most significant changes was in the setting of targets; by 2015, many of the retailers had moved away from annual targets to three- or five-year climate change and/or energy targets. Not only did this signal that they were thinking about climate change in a more strategic manner; they were also institutionalising climate change as an organisational priority and were committing to action over a longer period of time. It also suggested that they were locking in their climate change improvement processes, and – noting the comments above about the dependability and plausibility of corporate commitments – that companies would deliver on these targets even if the external pressures for action weakened. This is a particularly important finding as it suggests that internal governance processes can take on some of the heavy lifting when external pressures weaken. For example, if government policy changes (e.g. as we have seen in Australia in the period 2007 to 2015, or in the US with the election of President Trump), these commitments and associated internal governance commitments may mean that companies continue to take action over an extended period of time. Of course, such action will not continue indefinitely; there will almost inevitably be a point where the external incentives and pressures are simply too weak and the internal processes too exhausted for the company to maintain its commitment to action on climate change. While speculative, our sense is that this point is most likely to occur at the time when it comes to revising corporate objectives and targets or to setting new targets. This is why the setting of targets over at least five-year periods is so important, as such targets allow companies to get through at least one electoral cycle before they reach this crunch point.

The existence of internal governance processes does not, however, necessarily mean that retailers or other companies will respond to external pressures by deciding to significantly reduce their emissions or their energy consumption. The specific actions that they take will depend on a whole series of factors: management views on the strength (intensity) and duration of the external pressures, whether management sees climate change as an operational issue or as an issue of strategic importance, previous experience with energy and emission reduction efforts (in particular, whether these were seen as delivering value to the business), the range of energy-saving opportunities that are available to the business, and the relative importance assigned to environmental and climate change-related issues compared to other business issues. As we saw in Chapters 4 and 5, if companies see climate change as an operational issue, this perception will tend to attenuate or dampen the influence of external pressures. Conversely, if climate change is seen as a strategic value driver, companies are more likely to respond effectively and quickly to external governance pressures. Irrespective of where companies sit on this spectrum, we must again re-emphasise that the business case for action is the key determinant of action; companies will generally only invest capital in situations when there is a clear financial case for doing so, and there is limited evidence that they will in situations where the financial costs outweigh the financial benefits of such investments.

What do we know about the relationship between external and internal climate governance processes?

Our analysis points to two distinct differences in corporate actions or performance on climate change that can be attributed to variations in external and internal governance pressures. The first is that there is a clear relationship between higher energy prices and the rate of reduction of greenhouse gas emissions. When we compare the performance of US and UK retailers between 2000 and 2015, we see that US retailers averaged a 0.6% per annum reduction in their greenhouse gas emissions whereas the UK retailers achieved almost twice that, averaging a 1.1% per annum reduction in their greenhouse gas emissions. A similar finding emerges when we compare the emissions intensity of US and UK retailers. From interviews, much of this difference in performance can be attributed to differences in energy prices. A similar picture can be seen in the case of Australia. As discussed in Chapter 5, Australian electricity prices have been relatively low compared to other countries, with various studies suggesting that the rate of improvement in end-use energy efficiency in Australia from 1990 through to the early 2000s was about half the OECD average.

The second difference is that the manner in which companies understand and define their responsibilities towards climate change risks and, in turn, how they act on these, is strongly influenced by the external pressures on companies. In countries where the external pressures are perceived as strong or in countries where weak external pressures are reasonably well aligned, and where these pressures are of reasonable duration (specifically, they exist for a number of years), it is more likely that companies will see climate change as a strategic business value driver. In many ways, the UK retail sector is illustrative of the sorts of performance outcomes that might be achieved through the strengthening of external governance pressures. The high-profile political and media discussions about climate change in the period 2005 to 2007, coupled with a clear appetite on the part of the UK government to act on climate change, led to UK supermarkets seeing regulatory or policy action on climate change as inevitable and as a permanent characteristic of the business landscape. This, in turn, led to them setting long-term emission reduction targets. These pressures – together with company-specific factors such as previous experiences with reducing emissions in their own operations or the nature of the relationship with their agricultural produce suppliers – also led to them explicitly focusing on supply chain-related emissions and working with suppliers to reduce these emissions. In contrast, in countries where climate change-related pressures were weaker or where these pressures were seen as less important than other sustainability-related issues, companies were much less likely to see climate change as a strategic value driver. This is reflected in the targets that retailers in other countries set themselves, which tended to focus on energy efficiency rather than greenhouse gas emissions, emphasise relative rather than absolute performance, be relatively short-term, and focus on operational performance rather than wider supply chain and value chain-related emissions and impacts.

Could more be achieved?

One of the most interesting findings from our research is how little explicit pressure retailers faced from stakeholders to take action to reduce their greenhouse gas emissions. Across the period 2000 to 2015, it was striking how little use stakeholders made of the governance and accountability mechanisms that were available to them. To take one example, while many of the retailers provided extensive disclosures on their greenhouse gas emissions and climate change-related objectives and targets, stakeholders appear to have paid little attention to this information. Could more have been achieved? To answer this question, we will now look at how one particular stakeholder group, namely NGOs, used the governance instruments available to them.

We start by acknowledging that NGOs – most obviously in the UK but also in other jurisdictions – played an important role in encouraging retailers to take action on climate change. They raised awareness of climate change as a business issue, encouraged companies to report on their climate change performance, encouraged companies to set objectives and targets, and encouraged retailers to offer a variety of environmentally friendly products and services. These were all important contributions and helped reach the point where by 2008 or 2009 large retailers recognised climate change as a business issue and had developed the management systems and processes to respond effectively to future external climate change-related pressures. Despite all this, many of the interviewees for this project, in the business and NGO communities alike, were sceptical about the willingness or ability of NGOs to catalyse further action by companies, in particular at the corporate or strategic level. A number also questioned whether NGOs had a meaningful role to play in discussions about the climate change performance or expectations of companies.

When we interrogated these positions a bit more, a number of different themes emerged. The first was that of capture of the NGO agenda. We highlighted this in the case of the UK in Chapter 4 where we noted that companies were presenting NGO expectations as being closely aligned with the manner in which companies saw their responsibilities and objectives. This is most apparent in relation to the question of relative versus absolute performance, where NGO emphasis on the importance of energy efficiency was interpreted by companies as an endorsement of efficiency-oriented approaches to climate change.

The second theme was that the retailers' rhetoric and positioning on climate change made it more difficult for NGOs to campaign effectively. Companies that had identified climate change as a business priority were able to move the discussion from one of whether or not they should take action on climate change to one of what exactly they should do. This enabled the supermarkets to position climate change as a technical issue requiring technical expertise not necessarily available to NGOs in areas such as supply chain management. Not only did this allow companies to argue that NGOs did not have the expertise needed by business but it also allowed companies to position themselves at the centre of debates on sustainability, and to argue that it was companies that had the capacities, expertise and resources needed to effectively respond to sustainability issues such as climate change.

The third theme was that carbon disclosure had not delivered on its promise. Companies used carbon disclosure requirements such as the CDP as a means of framing the debate on climate change in terms that were most favourable to them. One way they did this was by emphasising relative rather than absolute performance. This framing builds on the assumption widely held by policymakers, investors and companies that good corporate management practices will inevitably lead to better performance (in terms of absolute GHG emissions) outcomes; this is despite the evidence from Doda et al. (2016) that such outcomes are unlikely unless companies express their targets in terms of the absolute GHG emission reductions they are looking to achieve (see, also, Dietz et al., 2018). Another way companies took control of the debate was by positioning companies as having the solutions to the issue of climate change, thereby making it harder for NGOs to challenge the legitimacy or credibility of the corporate response and, in turn, making it harder to demand further action. Furthermore, even allowing for this inevitable tendency for companies to present information in a way that shows them in the best possible light, the variations in the scope, coverage and consistency of carbon disclosure and reporting made it very difficult to compare corporate performance either over time or with other companies. The consequence was that corporate leaders were able to make ambitious statements on their commitments to action on climate change, knowing that it would be very difficult to hold them to account.

While we acknowledge these challenges, NGOs do need to take responsibility for much of this state of affairs. NGOs played an important role in getting companies to set objectives and targets and report on performance. However, they subsequently paid little attention to company narratives on climate change, to the quality of the information being reported, to the quality of the objectives and targets being set (e.g. how do they compare to those suggested by the IPCC) or to company performance against these objectives and targets. They, as a consequence, effectively allowed companies to set the terms of the debate and did not hold companies to account for their performance.

Our research identified three factors that were of particular importance in the period 2000 to 2015, and that continued to be of importance through to 2020. First, NGOs engaging with the retail sector did not maintain their focus on climate change but, instead, seemed to jump from issue to issue in the 15 years covered by our research. In this time, the high-profile NGO campaign topics ranged from recycling to palm oil, from organic food to human rights, from urban regeneration to wages, and from skills to climate change. This jumping from issue to issue reflected NGOs' need to collect money and consistently prove themselves to their donors and funders; it is often easier to raise money and generate media coverage for issues that are perceived as new and exciting rather than those that are more mature. It meant that companies did not receive a consistent and sustained message from NGOs on the importance of strong action on climate change, and led at least some companies to conclude that climate change was not an issue of strategic importance.

Second, carbon reporting is a highly technical area. Unpicking and understanding individual company data and performance (in terms of total emissions, in terms of performance against objectives and targets) is not an easy task. It requires knowledge of how companies generate and present data, the ability to critically analyse and interrogate these data (with companies often not providing enough information to enable stakeholders to verify these data), the ability to engage technically with the individuals that produce these data, and the time and resources to analyse and make sense of company data sets. These skills and resources were generally not present within the NGO community and accessing these skills (e.g. through consultancy firms) was often prohibitively expensive.

Third, the career needs and interests of the individuals charged with leading corporate engagement or campaigning often took them in a different direction to where where they needed to go if they were to deliver substantive change in company practice and performance. Analysing corporate data and performance was not seen as the glamorous end of campaigning and, given that many of these campaigners saw themselves as thought-leaders, it was not where they wanted to spend their time. This was compounded by the reality that even if weaknesses were found in companies' reporting or in their performance, it was difficult to translate these into high-profile media stories or campaign narratives.

These comments about why NGOs make such limited use of the levers that are available also apply to other private or civic actors. For example, investors also played an important role in encouraging companies to improve their reporting and to better manage climate change-related risks and opportunities. However, investors did not pay much attention to the quality of the information being reported, the quality of the targets being set or the outcomes being achieved. The reasons were similar to those identified for NGOs: the multiple issues on the responsible investment agenda, the constant search for new issues and the need for positive press coverage.

Is this important? The short answer is yes. If we acknowledge that – while not necessarily perfect – the commitments made by companies are likely to make a significant contribution to greenhouse gas emission reductions, it is then essential that companies are pressed to set meaningful and ambitious targets, to deliver on these targets, and that accountabilities and expectations are defined by reference to these targets. This pressure should also lead to companies recognising that climate change is a strategic value driver, not just another operational efficiency issue. In that context, the general lack of attention being paid by NGOs, investors and others as to whether companies are setting meaningful targets or are delivering against these targets is clearly a missed opportunity. In a context where the financial case for action may be limited and where other governance processes are weak, those levers that are available need to be used effectively. Put another way, NGOs and other stakeholders cannot just assume that the fact that a company has provided some disclosures and set some targets on climate change allows them to move on to other issues. In fact, our conclusion is that NGOs need to think much more carefully about how these commitments are to be implemented and to invest in building the capacities and tools necessary to hold companies to account for the delivery of these commitments.

Concluding comments: revisiting the coercive power of the state

Our research points to the important contribution that external governance pressures and internal governance conditions can make to delivering substantial improvements in corporate carbon and energy performance. These governance processes can put climate change on the corporate agenda; they can transform climate change from being seen as an operational issue to a strategic issue; they support the building of organisational capacity; they can lead to companies delivering substantial improvements in their own performance; and they can encourage companies to act on the greenhouse emissions associated with their supply chains and their wider value chains. These were, for the retail sector, and will be, for other sectors, important and valuable contributions to the wider goals of reducing global greenhouse gas emissions.

Yet, we also need to recognise that it is the business case for action – the costs of taking action, the financial benefits of taking action, the likelihood that energy prices will rise or fall over time (and by how much), the likelihood that government will intervene to raise (or lower) energy or carbon prices – which ultimately determines the actions that companies will take and the level of greenhouse gas emission reductions that will be seen. But if the business case weakens, or if the opportunities for incremental change are exhausted, the scope for further progress is likely to be restricted. The evidence from the retail sector in the period 2000 to 2015 – although we see no reason to assume that other sectors were any different – was that there were very few signs that any of the retailers were considering radical changes in their business models; certainly none of them seemed to see any alternative to business growth and the power of non-state actors to force them to consider such presumably unpalatable changes seemed to be very limited.

It is clear that markets alone cannot be relied upon to deliver the substantial cuts in greenhouse gas emissions necessary to minimise the likelihood of catastrophic climate change. In order to ensure that companies reduce their greenhouse gas emissions, governments need to establish a long-term policy framework that provides appropriate incentives and certainty. Within this, it is critical that energy and carbon prices remain sufficiently high for sufficiently long for companies to recognise that incrementalism is not a sufficient response to the climate emergency.

Within this stronger conception of the role of the state, private and civic actors and the influence they can exert are critical. They can ensure that companies are aware of the signals that are being sent, of their intent, their ambition and their duration. They can ensure that companies know how to interpret these signals, and that companies have the management competencies that they need to respond effectively. They can amplify and reinforce these pressures through encouraging companies to set and deliver appropriately demanding and outcome-oriented (i.e. focused on absolute rather than relative performance) long-term targets, holding them to account if they do not deliver, and praising them if they do deliver. And what about companies themselves? They can ensure that their internal governance processes are fit for purpose and that they can recognise and respond effectively to the external governance pressures that they face, thereby ensuring that their companies are successful and sustainable over the long term.

Appendix 1
Some notes on methods and data

Assessing the performance of new forms of governance

Approaches to policy evaluation are well established and have been applied in multiple domains for many years. Established communities of policy analysts employ a range of standard methods and can often access diverse and reasonably reliable data sets to assess the performance of specific policy interventions and broader policy frameworks, and the interactions between policy interventions and policy frameworks. In contrast, despite the existence of substantial literature on the governance of corporations, similar literature on performance assessment has not yet emerged or coalesced in the governance field.

The challenges of governance evaluation

Governance interventions can come from multiple actors at different levels in various policy domains. They can involve a wide range of actors, and governance frameworks in multiple domains can interact in complex ways. The boundaries between different frameworks and between public, private and civic forms of governance are not always clear; we often see hybrid forms of governance that are highly idiosyncratic or unique to a particular time and place. Although some forms of governance have been formalised, and therefore made relatively amenable to scrutiny, many forms of governance are highly informal, fluid and opaque. Many actors, particularly private and civic actors, rarely announce their initiatives, they may not be clear or open about their goals, the approaches that they use or the ways in which they apply them. Their approaches can change rapidly and regularly with new initiatives emerging in unannounced and uncoordinated ways. Governance initiatives can slowly fade away as a result of, for example. the actors that supported their creation not maintaining interest, or because the pressures for action have waned.

To further compound these issues, the external pressures or influences from public, private or civic actors interact with the internal conditions within the targets of the governance intervention to shape outcomes and contributions to or impacts on the public interest. For corporations, these internal conditions – which may relate to their leadership and cultures, structures and systems and the different resource endowments that they can mobilise – help the organisation to detect, make sense of and decide how to respond to the wide range of external influences that they are subjected to. Furthermore, it is unlikely that corporations or any other target of a governance intervention will be the passive recipients of external pressure. Instead, they are likely to attempt to influence the conditions within they operate, and to deflect, dilute or discount the pressures that they are subjected to.

Outcomes vary according to the ways in which external pressures and internal conditions interact. And these interactions can be highly reflexive; different actors can anticipate and respond not only to an actual governance intervention but also to the prospect of an intervention so that the behaviour of one actor is shaped by the anticipated behaviour of another. Evaluation must therefore consider not only the governance conditions in place, but also those that the different actors think could be put into place and those that the actors previously thought could or might be put in place.

The end result is that it is often difficult to understand how external governance pressures influence corporate behaviour and how these pressures, in turn, both shape and are shaped by the behaviour and performance of corporations. These factors pose problems for any attempt at evaluation. They mean that governance interventions relating to corporations are often not readily amenable to evaluation except on an in-depth and case-by-case basis. Evaluation depends on analysts having time, resources and access to detailed information and in-depth understanding of conditions within corporations.

The potential of bottom-up approaches

So which methods might work to enable us to say more about the potential of new forms of governance? There are different ways in which we could start to strengthen the evidence base on the performance of different forms of governance. Top-down analysis starts with a particular governance intervention – a government policy, an investor engagement, an NGO campaign for example – and tries to trace its impact through the organisations that are the target of the intervention and to the outcomes or impacts that result. This is attractive and is often called for as particular actors want to understand the influence of specific interventions. However, disentangling the influence of one intervention from those of a myriad of other factors is very difficult. There is a high risk of attributing influence inappropriately and of ignoring other important influences and contingencies.

In contrast, bottom-up approaches that start with an outcome and then work backwards to identify the relative significance of a wide range of different influences are often more viable and appropriate. They approach the issue by identifying a particular aspect of corporate behaviour or performance and then working back to understand the relative significance of the wide range of factors that give rise to it. Rather than focusing on the influence or impact of one governance intervention – an assessment of the influence of a particular policy, investment or NGO campaign for example – the bottom-up approach considers the combined influence of many governance interventions. In other words, it takes the broader governance framework rather than a specific governance intervention as its primary unit of analysis. Although it assesses the combined effect of the framework as a whole, it can also offer valuable insights into the relative importance of specific actors or governance interventions within that framework.

How have we assessed the governance in this research?

The main questions considered in this book are whether, to what extent and under what conditions new forms of governance can ensure that corporations make a fuller contribution to the realisation of public interest objectives. Given the relative lack of evidence on actual outcomes and the limits of top-down approaches discussed above, we conducted a detailed bottom-up empirical investigation into how a key sector is responding to a critically important public interest objective. Below we discuss some of the methodological and other considerations relevant to the research.

Why focus on the retail sector?

The retail sector is one of the largest commercial sectors in many countries. It is estimated that the retail sector accounts for 8% of GDP in the United States and 14% in India, and that the retail and wholesale trade is the third largest economic sector in Germany, accounting for 9.4% of total gross value added (Luce, 2013: 3). The sector's contribution to employment is similarly large with retail employment accounting for 10 to 15% of total employment in many countries (Luce, 2013: 4).

Despite the scale of its economic and employment footprint, retailers may seem a somewhat unlikely subject for an analysis of the governance of corporate responses to climate change. Unlike, for example, mining, oil and gas or electricity companies, they are not obvious polluters; retailers don't have tall stacks discharging pollutants and are generally located in reasonably well-kept buildings. In fact, they could just as easily be characterised by their unobtrusiveness, cleanliness and silence. Furthermore, it is not clear that there is any particular need to regulate their environmental impacts. Retailers tend to rely on electricity and gas to provide most of their heating and lighting, they tend to have reasonably modern and efficient vehicle fleets, and they bear no obvious responsibility for the environmental impacts of their supply chain.

A closer look at the sector suggests that, perhaps contrary to what might be expected, the sector's greenhouse gas emissions are significant. It is estimated that UK supermarkets (through their own operations and their electricity consumption – through the use of lighting, heating, cold stores and on-shelf refrigeration) account for 0.9% of the UK's total greenhouse gas emissions (SDC, 2008: 40). A similar picture emerges from the United States, where it is estimated that the US retail sector accounts for the largest energy bill and the second largest amount of greenhouse gas emissions in the entire commercial sector of the US economy (RILA, 2012: 14).

Even though these operational emissions are large, they are dwarfed by the emissions from elsewhere in their supply chain and value chains. For UK supermarkets, greenhouse gas emissions from their food chains – agricultural inputs, food manufacture, transport, storage, distribution, refrigeration and packaging, home cooking – are estimated to be an order of magnitude greater than those associated with their direct operations (SDC, 2008: 40). Some companies have tried to quantify these emissions. The UK retailer Tesco estimated that the emissions from its UK supply chain were approximately ten times its direct operational emissions (Tesco, 2010: 14), and US retailer Walmart suggested that its supply chain was likely to have annual greenhouse gas emissions that were at least 100 times greater than its operational emissions (Walmart, 2009b). Of course, it could be argued that – at least in a strict legal sense – retailers do not have formal responsibility for the greenhouse gas emissions associated with the products that they sell or for the manner in which the products are subsequently used or consumed by their customers. However, as we discuss in Chapters 4 and 5, some retailers have acknowledged that they do have at least some responsibility for these emissions. They have sought to influence these emissions through, for example, requiring their suppliers to report on their greenhouse gas emissions or to set greenhouse gas emission reduction targets; through providing technical or other support to suppliers looking to reduce their emissions; and through educating customers on the actions that they could take to reduce emissions in their daily lives. As such, we concluded that supply chain-related emissions and actions directed at managing these emissions were clearly within the scope of our research.

The scale and scope of the sector is therefore enormous. However, when it comes to climate change, the sector is not governed in the same way as sectors such as oil and gas or automobile, which are the subject of multiple forms of state-based policies and regulations. In fact, despite the size of their carbon footprint, retailers are generally not directly regulated by government; there has, of course, been regulation in certain areas such as building energy efficiency and transport (or vehicle efficiency), but these regulations have, generally, not been targeted specifically at the retail sector. The emissions from the retail sector are also shaped by a range of other economic, information-based and voluntary forms of policy. Retailers are both the source and the objects of numerous other non-state governance pressures; they govern themselves, their supply chains and the choices and impacts of their customers, but they are also governed by market conditions, societal expectations, media representations, customer concerns, various private standards and voluntary codes and so on.

From a business perspective, the retail sector is actually quite representative of many other sectors. Many companies in other sectors have characteristics – for example, significant operational and supply chain-related emissions, long and complex supply chains, and extensive interaction with and influence on customers and suppliers – that are similar to companies in the retail sector. The retail sector therefore potentially provides important insights into the wider role that different forms of governance can play in influencing corporate practice and performance.

Scope

In this book, we focus our attention in two areas. In Chapter 4 we analyse the UK supermarket sector's approach to climate change. The UK is one of the world's largest retail markets and UK supermarkets have long been recognised as leaders for their approach to climate change and corporate responsibility more generally. The UK, therefore, provides important insights into 'the art of the possible' and the limits of what might be achieved. In Chapter 5, we look at the climate change practices and performances of the world's 25 largest retailers, and compare these to those of the UK supermarket sector. Apart from their scale, most of these retailers now provide a detailed account of their climate change-related policies, objectives and targets, actions, and performance outcomes, and of the drivers for action on climate change. This reporting allows factors such as the influence of national regulation, the influence of energy prices, the role of internal governance factors, and cultures and beliefs on corporate action to be analysed.

Research approach

Our analysis of the climate change performance and actions of the global retail sector involved three main activities.

First, we identified a number of standard performance measures (e.g. total greenhouse gas emissions, energy intensity) that we could use to track the performance of individual companies over time and that we could use to make meaningful comparisons between companies.

Second, we conducted a detailed content and data analysis of the information presented in each company's corporate responsibility (or equivalent) reports, their responses to the CDP[1] (previously the Carbon Disclosure Project), their annual reports, and their other published materials. Our analysis covered publications from the late 1990s (when the first corporate responsibility reports were produced) through to the end of 2016 (which included data and analysis through to the end of 2015). This meant that, for some companies, we had over 15 corporate responsibility reports to review. Some companies also published reports specific to their operations in particular countries (e.g. Asda, part of the Walmart group, published a number of reports on its greenhouse gas emissions and on its climate change strategy). In total, we reviewed over 270 corporate responsibility, sustainability and climate change-related reports, over 100 CDP responses, 25 corporate websites, and many more country and product-specific websites and materials.

We supplemented this literature review with some 30 interviews with retailers in each of the countries reviewed, peak industry bodies, non-governmental organisations and consumer groups, and other stakeholders. These interviews focused on the drivers for corporate action on climate change and energy-related issues, and the manner in which these drivers had influenced internal governance processes and corporate actions on climate change. The desktop review and interviews enabled us to determine when climate change and energy-related issues appeared on the corporate agenda, to track the evolution of companies' policies, actions and targets on climate change and energy-related issues, and to track companies' climate change and energy performance over time.

Even though companies differed in terms of the specific information provided, the majority provided information on their energy greenhouse gas emission management systems and processes, their greenhouse gas emissions, their objectives and targets, the actions they had taken to meet these objectives and targets, and their performance against these objectives. These elements allowed us to develop time series of how companies' energy and climate change performance, in both absolute and relative (efficiency) terms, had evolved over time. They also allowed us to determine when climate change and energy-related issues appeared on the corporate agenda, to track the evolution of companies' policies, actions and targets on climate change and energy-related issues, and to identify the drivers (or motivations) for these companies to take action on climate change.

Third, we conducted interviews with the corporate responsibility managers (or equivalent) and other operational managers of many of these companies. These interviews focused on: the actions they had taken, how the actions taken had evolved over time, their objectives and targets and their performance against these, the drivers (internal and external) for action and how the drivers had influenced the actions taken, and their views on the dependability of the commitments they have made. We supplemented these with a series of stakeholder and expert interviews to better understand the wider context within which these companies were operating and to understand the factors that influenced these companies' climate change strategies and actions.

Finally, we presented and obtained feedback on initial findings at a series of industry conferences and to key stakeholder groups over the period 2010 to 2015. These included presentations to the International Energy Agency and the Department of Energy and Climate Change (UK), and conferences in various countries including the UK, Australia, France and India.

Data quality and availability: some critical reflections

The quality, quantity and breadth of coverage of the information provided in corporate responsibility and other reports had, as we discuss below, significant implications for our research and, as we discuss elsewhere in this book, profound implications for wider governance processes. We note that data and data quality has been a major focus of our research over the past 20 years. We have written specifically on data from a policy design and implementation perspective (see Gouldson, 2004; Gouldson and Sullivan, 2007; Kolominskas and Sullivan, 2004;

Sullivan, 2009, 2010, 2011a; Sullivan and Gouldson, 2007, 2012; Sullivan and Woods, 2000), and on data in the context of the retail sector (see Gouldson and Sullivan, 2013, 2014; Sullivan and Gouldson, 2013, 2017, 2017) and in other sectors (see Dietz et al., 2018; Doda et al., 2016; Sullivan (2005).

Despite the huge volume of material that was published between 2000 and 2015, there were significant limitations in the data and information provided.

First, while almost all of the 30 retailers covered by our research provided at least some basic information on their approach to climate change, not all provided performance data. More specifically, 6 out of the 30 companies covered did not provide any quantitative information at any point in this 15-year period on historic emissions performance, current emissions or on expected future performance.

Second, retailers reported over different time periods. While some had greenhouse gas emissions data extending back to the late 1990s, others only started to report quantitative data in more recent years. For example, Lowe's Corporation issued its first corporate responsibility report in 2004, but only published its first greenhouse gas emissions inventory in 2012.

Third, many of the retailers covered by our research restated or revised their data over time. In fact, a number restated or revised their historic data almost every year! The restating of data should not be treated as suspicious or as a sign that companies are looking to hide something. There are practical reasons why emissions data needs to be restated. These can include internal factors such as improvements in company data gathering and acquisition processes, changes in the manner in which emissions are calculated, changes in the scope of reporting, and business changes such as acquisitions and the in-sourcing or out-sourcing of particular business functions. The reasons can also include external factors such as changes in standard emission factors for grid-based electricity, the evolution of reporting protocols such as the CDP, and the introduction of formal regulatory requirements which often prescribe how data are to be calculated and reported. We should note that many of the companies covered by our research did correct at least some of their historic data. However, these revisions tended to be confined to the most recent three- or five-years' worth of data, rather than covering the entire period for which the company had reported. This limited our ability to understand the longer-term trends in companies' emissions profiles (or to understand whether emissions had, in fact, increased or decreased).

Fourth, while reporting on operational emissions (i.e. emissions from building energy use, refrigeration, transport) was reasonably well established in the retail sector by 2010 or 2011, there was limited reporting on supply chain, consumer and product-related emissions even in 2015.

Fifth, the qualitative information provided by retailers tended to be that which created the best impression of the company's practices and performance (Sullivan, 2011a: 59–90). Most of the retailers, inevitably, focused most attention on their successes, the targets that had been met and on good news case-studies. They tended to pay correspondingly less attention to areas where things did not go so well, to targets that had not been achieved (or to the reasons why targets have not been achieved) or to performance data that did not support a narrative of continuous improvement.

Sixth, there was a general lack of technical analysis of the data being reported (e.g. on the technical details of their emissions calculations such as the specific emissions factors used and the emissions calculation protocols used) and on the factors that had influenced the performance outcomes that were reported (e.g. the effectiveness of specific emission reductions initiatives, the effect of changes in the approach to reporting, the effect of wider changes in the business).

It is important to acknowledge that these limitations are not unique to the retail sector. In fact, the limitations in corporate environmental and climate change reporting, and the consequences for the structure and content of the dialogue between companies and stakeholders, are well recognised (Milne and Grubnic, 2011; Unerman and Bennett, 2004). Addressing these sorts of issues is one of the most long-running themes in the environmental accounting literature (Schaltegger, 1997).

Many of these issues persist and the same criticisms could be levelled at much of the corporate reporting that is provided in 2020. However, there has been progress, with the CDP playing a particularly important role. While the CDP is a voluntary reporting requirement and only applies to listed companies, the strong support provided by investors and the large number of companies that report to the CDP mean that it plays an important role in framing corporate climate change reporting. In recent years, the CDP has strengthened its focus on data quality, asking companies to explain why and how their emissions have changed (and, specifically, whether changes are due to business growth, recalculations, or the company's actions to reduce GHG emissions). In addition, the CDP publishes a Carbon Disclosure Leadership Index that ranks companies on the quality and completeness of their disclosures.

The implications for our research

The limitations in the data provided by companies had a number of implications for our research. The most important was that it limited our ability to compare the performance of different companies, even those within a particular geographic region or those that, by virtue of their activities, could be considered directly comparable. That is, notwithstanding the volume of data available, we did not feel that we could develop a credible ranking or benchmark of company performance on climate change. Furthermore, while we were able to make some very broad estimates of the significance of the sector's operational emissions compared to, for example, national greenhouse gas emissions, the data were not sufficiently robust to enable us to develop a credible estimate of the total emissions from the 30 companies covered in our research. In addition, while the quality of the supplementary information being provided by companies improved over the period researched, it was difficult to assess the effectiveness of company greenhouse gas emission reduction efforts.

For example, if a company reported a reduction in its greenhouse gas emissions from energy use, it was very difficult to assess whether the reported changes were due to an actual reduction in energy use, fuel shifting (towards lower carbon intensity fuels), changes in calculation methodologies (e.g. new emission factors) or some combination of these factors.

We were, however, able to use the data in a number of ways. We found that companies that had reported for five or more years, and so had reached a certain maturity in their reporting efforts, tended to be reasonably consistent in terms of the scope of their reporting, the data used, the performance indicators used, and the assumptions made. This allowed us to make reasonably robust assessments of the trends in each individual company's operational performance in both absolute and relative (efficiency) terms, of its performance against its own objectives and targets, and of the quality of its implementation of its climate change strategy. However, we were unable to do the same for the emissions associated with supply chains and value chains.

The reported information enabled us to track the evolution of corporate strategies – including overarching policies, objectives and targets, actions – on climate change at both the aggregate and the individual company level. The fact that many of the companies covered by our research had been producing corporate responsibility reports for a number of years before they started to talk explicitly about climate change meant that we were able to identify the point when climate change appeared on the corporate agenda and/or the point where companies felt sufficiently emboldened or sufficiently pressurised to talk publicly about the issue. Of course, the introduction of an issue in a corporate responsibility report does not necessarily correspond to the point where an issue appeared on the corporate agenda. In some companies, the inclusion of information in a corporate responsibility report is very much the final part of a process, i.e. these companies only report when they have decided on their strategies and actions. Others, in contrast, can introduce topics in their reports ahead of being in a position to actually take action on the issue in question. Our interviews with the corporate responsibility (or equivalent) and other operational managers of the companies covered by our research provided us with further insights into the timing of corporate responses and actions, both in terms of when issues first appeared on the corporate agenda and of when specific actions were taken.

These interviews also allowed us to develop a robust understanding of the motivations or drivers for action. Corporate responsibility reporting provides some insights, although the retailers, reflecting the shareholder orientation of many of their communications on environmental and social issues, tended to emphasise cost avoidance and responding to consumer interests, even in situations where there are clearly other factors at play. Our interviews with the companies allowed us dig deeper and provided us with a deeper understanding of the actions companies had taken, how these actions taken had evolved over time, their objectives and targets, their performance against these objectives and targets, and the drivers for action.

Note

1 CDP is an investor-backed initiative that, annually, requests information on the risks and opportunities of climate change from the world's largest companies. This information – individual company responses, as well as a series of country, region and issue-specific reports – is made available through the CDP's website. See further: www.cdp.net/en.

Appendix 2

About CCCEP and the climate governance beyond the state project

About CCCEP

The ESRC Centre for Climate Change Economics and Policy (CCCEP) brings together some of the world's leading researchers on climate change economics and policy, from many different disciplines. It was established in 2008 and its third phase began on 1 October 2018. The Centre is also a member of the Place-based Climate Action Network (P-CAN), which was launched on 31 January 2019.

The Centre is hosted jointly by the University of Leeds and the London School of Economics and Political Science (LSE) and is chaired by Professor Lord Stern of Brentford. It is funded by the Economic and Social Research Council (ESRC).

The Centre's mission is to advance public and private action on climate change through rigorous, innovative research.

Research objectives

Phase 3 of the Centre consists of seven projects, as follows:

- Low-carbon, climate-resilient cities
- Sustainable infrastructure finance
- Low-carbon industrial strategies in challenging contexts
- Integrating climate and development policies for 'climate-compatible development'
- Competitiveness in the low-carbon economy
- Incentives for behaviour change
- Climate information for adaptation

They build on the five research themes during Phase 2 – understanding green growth and climate-compatible development, advancing climate finance and investment, evaluating the performance of climate policies, managing climate risks and uncertainties and strengthening climate services, and enabling rapid transitions in mitigation and adaptation – and complement other projects carried out at the Grantham Research Institute on Climate Change and the Environment and the London School of Economics and Political Science, and at the School of Earth and Environment at the University of Leeds.

Funding

The Centre for Climate Change Economics and Policy has been funded since its foundation in 2008 by the UK Economic and Social Research Council. Phase 1 of funding was provided from October 2008 until September 2013, and support for Phase 2 occurred between October 2013 and September 2018. Phase 3 of funding began on 1 October 2018.

Climate governance beyond the state? Corporations and the transition to a low-carbon economy

One of the projects undertaken under the Climate Change Governance for a New Global Deal programme focused on corporations and the transition to a low-carbon economy. The project, which was led by Dr Rory Sullivan and Professor Andy Gouldson, ran from 2010 to 2015. This book is based on the research from that project.

The project examined how corporate climate change performance has been influenced by non-state actors (NGOs, investors, employees, customers, etc). The project sought to understand:

- The factors – external and internal to the organisation – that have influenced corporate climate change performance;
- The extent to which these influence corporate behaviour and, specifically, how far they can move companies beyond the actions that are required by legislation or that would be justified in narrow cost-benefit terms.

From a climate change perspective, the objectives were to understand how these interventions work and how effective they are, or could be, in moving us towards the goals of a low-carbon economy and, based on this analysis, to offer proposals on the public policy frameworks that need to be in place to facilitate or accelerate these changes and to make the non-state interventions more effective.

While the retail sector was the primary focus, the project also explored wider questions about the origins and influence of different forms of governance, and around how corporate actions can be directed towards ends that are socially and environmentally sustainable.

Major publications from the project

Doda, B., Gennaioli, C., Gouldson, A., Grover, D. and Sullivan, R. (2016), 'Are Corporate Carbon Management Practices Reducing Corporate Carbon Emissions?', *Corporate Social Responsibility and Environmental Management*, Vol. 23, pp. 257–270.

Gouldson, A. and Sullivan, R. (2012), 'Ecological Modernisation and the Spaces for Feasible Action on Climate Change', in Pelling, M., Manuel-Navarrete, D. & Redclift, M. (eds.), *Climate Change and the Crisis of Capitalism* (Routledge, Abingdon, UK), pp. 114–125.

Gouldson, A. and Sullivan, R. (2013), 'Long-term Corporate Climate Change Targets: What Could They Deliver?', *Environmental Science & Policy*, 27 (March 2013), pp. 1–10.

Gouldson, A. and Sullivan, R. (2014), 'Understanding the Governance of Corporations: An Examination of the Factors Shaping UK Supermarket Strategies on Climate Change', *Environment and Planning A*, Vol. 46, No. 12, pp. 2972–2990.

Gouldson, A., Sullivan, R. and Afionis, S. (2014), 'Corporate Social Responsibility, Sustainability and the Governance of Business', in Atkinson, G., Dietz, S., Neumayer, E. & Agarwala, M. (eds.), *Handbook of Sustainable Development. Second Edition* (Edward Elgar, Cheltenham), pp. 564–576.

Sullivan, R. and Gouldson, A. (2012), 'Does Voluntary Carbon Reporting Meet Investors' Needs?', *Journal of Cleaner Production*, Vol. 36, pp. 60–67.

Sullivan, R. and Gouldson, A. (2013), 'Ten Years of Corporate Action on Climate Change: What Do We Have To Show For It?', *Energy Policy*, Vol. 60, pp. 733–740.

Sullivan, R. and Gouldson, A. (2016), 'Comparing the Climate Change Actions, Targets and Performance of UK and US Retailers', *CSR and Environmental Management*, Volume 23, No. 3, pp. 129–139.

Sullivan, R. and Gouldson, A. (2017), 'The Governance of Corporate Responses to Climate Change: An International Comparison', *Business Strategy and the Environment*, Vol. 26, pp. 413–425.

References

Aeon (2001), *Aeon Environmental Report 2001* (Aeon, Chiba).

Aeon (2002), *Aeon Environmental Report 2002* (Aeon, Chiba).

Aeon (2003), *Aeon Environmental and Social Report 2003* (Aeon, Chiba).

Aeon (2004), *Aeon Environmental and Social Report 2004* (Aeon, Chiba).

Aeon (2005), *Aeon Environmental and Social Report 2005* (Aeon, Chiba).

Aeon (2006), *Aeon Environmental and Social Report 2006* (Aeon, Chiba).

Aeon (2007), *Aeon Environmental and Social Report 2007* (Aeon, Chiba).

Aeon (2008a), *Aeon Environmental and Social Report 2008* (Aeon, Chiba).

Aeon (2008b), 'Aeon's Response to the 2008 CDP Survey' (Aeon, Chiba).

Aeon (2009a), *Aeon Environmental and Social Report 2009* (Aeon, Chiba).

Aeon (2009b), *Aeon Environmental and Social Report 2009: Data Pages* (Aeon, Chiba).

Aeon (2010), *Aeon Environmental and Social Report 2010* (Aeon, Chiba).

Aeon (2011), *Aeon Environmental and Social Report 2011* (Aeon, Chiba).

Aeon (2012a), *Aeon Environmental and Social Report 2012* (Aeon, Chiba).

Aeon (2012b), 'Aeon's Response to the 2012 CDP Survey' (Aeon, Chiba).

Aeon (2013), *Aeon Environmental and Social Report 2013* (Aeon, Chiba).

Aldi (2011a), 'Energy Saving' (Aldi, Mülheim an der Ruhr).

Aldi (2014a), 'Efficient Low-impact Operations' (Aldi, Mülheim an der Ruhr).

Aldi (2014b), 'Green Buildings' (Aldi, Mülheim an der Ruhr).

Aldi (2014c), 'Use Alternative Energies' (Aldi, Mülheim an der Ruhr).

Aldi (2014d), 'Energy-saving and Carbon Neutral Cooled' (Aldi, Mülheim an der Ruhr).

Amos, N. and Sullivan, R. (2018), *The Business of Farm Animal Welfare* (Routledge, Abingdon).

Andriof, J. (2002), *Unfolding Stakeholder Thinking: Theory, Responsibility and Engagement* (Greenleaf, Sheffield).

Asda (2013a), *Sustainability Policy and Targets to 2015* (Asda, Weybridge).

Asda (2013b), *Asda's Carbon Footprint 2012* (Asda, Weybridge).

Australian Bureau of Statistics (2012), '1301.0 – Year Book Australia, 2012' (Australian Bureau of Statistics, Canberra).

Australian Food and Grocery Council (AFGC) (2014), 'Media Release: Carbon Tax Repeal is Good News for Food and Grocery Manufacturing. 17 July 2014' (AFGC, Canberra).

Australian Food and Grocery Council (AFGC) and A.T. Kearney Australia (2011), *2020: Industry at Crossroads* (AFGC, Canberra).

Australian National Retailers' Association (ANRA) (2014), 'Press Release: Supermarkets Continue to Put Consumers First in Carbon Debate. 17 July 2014' (ANRA, Canberra).

Australian Retailers Association (ARA) (2014), 'Press Release: Retailers Celebrate Carbon Tax Removal – A Victory for Retailers, Consumers and Common Sense. 17 July 2014' (ARA, Barton, ACT).

Ayres, I. and Braithwaite, J. (1992), *Responsive Regulation: Transcending the Deregulation Debate* (Oxford University Press, Oxford).

Bache, I. and Flinders, M. (eds) (2005). *Multi-level Governance* (Oxford University Press, Oxford).

Barney, J. (2001) 'Is the Resource Based Theory a Useful Perspective for Strategic Management Research? Yes', *Academy of Management Review*, Vol. 26, No. 1, pp. 41–56.

BBC (2019), *Climategate: Science of a Scandal* (2019), BBC Four (14 November 2019).

Best Buy (2013), *Fiscal 2014 Sustainability Report* (Best Buy, Richfield, MN).

Best Buy (2014), *Fiscal 2014 Sustainability Report* (Best Buy, Richfield, MN).

Black, J. (2008), 'Constructing and Contesting Legitimacy and Accountability in Polycentric Regulatory Regimes', *Regulation and Governance*, Vol. 2, No. 2, pp. 137–164.

Bleher, D. (2013), *The Future Impact of CSR in the Food Sector on Climate Change. IMPACT Working Paper No. 18* (csrIMPACT, Brussels).

Bouwen, P. (2004), 'Exchanging Access Goods for Access: A Comparative Study of Business Lobbying in the European Union Institutions', *European Journal of Political Research*, Vol. 43, No. 3, pp. 337–369.

Boyd, R., Cranston-Turner, J. and Ward, B. (2015), *Tracking Intended Nationally Determined Contributions: What are the Implications for Greenhouse Gas Emissions in 2030? August 2015* (Centre for Climate Change Economics and Policy, London).

Boyd, R., Stern, N. and Ward, B. (2015), *What Will Global Annual Emissions of Greenhouse Gases be in 2030, and Will They be Consistent with Avoiding Global Warming of More Than 2°C? May 2015* (Centre for Climate Change Economics and Policy, London).

British Retail Consortium (2009), *A Better Retailing Climate. Progress Report 2009* (British Retail Consortium, London).

British Retail Consortium (2010), *A Better Retailing Climate. Progress Report 2010* (British Retail Consortium, London).

British Retail Consortium (2012), *A Better Retailing Climate. Towards Sustainable Retail* (British Retail Consortium, London).

British Retail Consortium (2013), *A Better Retailing Climate. Progress Report 2012* (British Retail Consortium, London).

British Retail Consortium (2014), *A Better Retailing Climate. Driving Resource Efficiency* (British Retail Consortium, London).

Busch, L. (2013) *Standards: Recipes for Reality* (MIT Press, Boston).

Business Roundtable (2019), 'Statement on the Purpose of a Corporation. 19 August 2019' (Business Roundtable, Washington DC).

Cadbury Committee (1992), *The Financial Elements of Corporate Governance* (Gee Publishing, London).

Carbon + Energy Markets (2012), *Electricity Prices in Australia: An International Comparison. A Report to the Energy Users Association of Australia* (Carbon + Energy Markets, Melbourne).

Carbon Disclosure Project (CDP) (2009), *Carbon Disclosure Project 2009: Japan 500 Report* (CDP, London).

Carbon Disclosure Project [CDP] (2010), *Carbon Disclosure Project 2010: Japan 500 Report* (CDP, London).

Carbon Disclosure Project [CDP] (2011), *CDP Japan 500 Report 2011* (CDP, London).

Carbon Disclosure Project [CDP] (2013a), *Global 500 Climate Change Report 2013* (CDP, London).

Carbon Disclosure Project [CDP] (2013b), *CDP S&P 500 Climate Change Report 2013* (CDP, London).

Carrefour (2005), *Sustainability Report 2004* (Carrefour, Paris).

Carrefour (2007), *Carrefour Group and Sustainable Development: Our Responses to 6 Major Issues* (Carrefour, Paris).

Carrefour (2008), *Carrefour Group Building Responsible Relationships. Sustainability Report 2007* (Carrefour, Paris).

Carrefour (2009a), 'At the Heart of Global Issues' (Carrefour, Paris).

Carrefour (2009b), *At the Heart of Life: 2008 Sustainability Report* (Carrefour, Paris).

Carrefour (2010a), *Annual Activity and Sustainability Report 2009* (Carrefour, Paris).

Carrefour (2010b), 'Response to the 2010 CDP Investor Information Request' (Carrefour, Paris).

Carrefour (2011), *2010 Expert Report; Sustainable Development at Carrefour* (Carrefour, Paris).

Carrefour (2012a), *2011 Annual Activity and Sustainability Report* (Carrefour, Paris).

Carrefour (2012b), 'Response to the 2012 CDP Investor Information Request' (Carrefour, Paris).

Carrefour (2013), *2012 Annual Activity and Responsible Commitment Report* (Carrefour, Paris).

Carrefour (2014), *2013 Annual Activity and Responsible Commitment Report* (Carrefour, Paris).

Chesebrough, D. and Sullivan, R. (2017), *Coping, Shifting, Changing 2.0: Corporate and Investor Strategies for Managing Market Short-termism* (UN Global Compact and Principles for Responsible Investment, London).

Coles (2014), 'Coles has Undertaken Significant Work to Improve Sustainability in our Supply Chain' (Coles, Hawthorn East).

Commonwealth of Australia (2004), *Securing Australia's Energy Future* (Commonwealth of Australia, Canberra).

Commonwealth of Australia (2011), *Securing A Clean Energy Future* (Commonwealth of Australia, Canberra).

Co-operative Group (2006), *The Co-operative Group: Sustainability Report 2005* (The Co-operative Group, Manchester).

Co-operative Group (2007), *Sustainability Report 2006* (The Co-operative Group, Manchester).

Co-operative Group (2008), *The Co-operative Sustainability Report 2007/08* (The Co-operative Group, Manchester).

Co-operative Group (2009), *Sustainability Report 2008/09* (The Co-operative Group, Manchester).

Co-operative Group (2011a), *Leading the Way: A Revolutionary Approach to Social Responsibility. Ethical Operating Plan (2011–2013)* (The Co-operative Group, Manchester).

Co-operative Group (2011b), *Sustainability Report 2010: Join the Revolution* (The Co-operative Group, Manchester).

Co-operative Group (2013a), *Our Ethical Plan 2013–2015* (The Co-operative Group, Manchester).

Co-operative Group (2013b), *Sustainability Report 2012: Building a Better Society* (The Co-operative Group, Manchester).

Costco (2009), *Corporate Sustainability Report. January 2009* (Costco Wholesale, Issaquah, WA, USA).

Costco (2011), *Annual Report 2011* (Costco Wholesale, Issaquah, WA).

Costco (2012a), *Sustainability FY 2012* (Costco Wholesale, Issaquah, WA).

Costco (2012b), 'Costco's Response to the 2012 CDP Survey' (Costco Wholesale, Issaquah, WA).

CVS Caremark (2012), *2011 Corporate Social Responsibility Report* (CVS Caremark, Woonsocket, RI).

CVS Caremark (2013), *2012 Corporate Social Responsibility Report* (CVS Caremark, Woonsocket, RI).

CVS Caremark (2014), *2013 Corporate Social Responsibility Report* (CVS Caremark, Woonsocket, RI).

DECC (2014), *Quarterly Energy Prices. December 2014* (DECC, London).

Deloitte (2012), *Global Powers of Retailing 2012* (Deloitte, London).

Deloitte (2014), *Global Powers of Retailing 2012* (Deloitte, London).

Department of Energy and Climate Change [DECC] (2012), 'Climate Change Act 2008' (DECC, London).

Dietz, S., Fruitiere, C., Garcia-Manas, C., Irwin, W., Rauis, B. and Sullivan, R. (2018), 'An Assessment of Climate Action by High-carbon Global Corporations', *Nature Climate Change*, Vol. 8, pp. 1072–1075.

Doda, B., Gennaioli, C., Gouldson, A., Grover, D. and Sullivan, R. (2016), 'Are Corporate Carbon Management Practices Reducing Corporate Carbon Emissions?', *Corporate Social Responsibility and Environmental Management*, Vol. 23, pp. 257–270.

Dyllick, T. and Hockerts, K. (2002), 'Beyond the Business Case for Corporate Sustainability', *Business Strategy and the Environment*, Vol. 11, pp. 130–141.

Edeka (2014a), 'Together for Climate Protection' (Edeka, Hamburg).

Edeka (2014b), 'Transport and Logistics' (Edeka, Hamburg).

Egels-Zanden, N. and Hyllman, P. (2006), 'Exploring the Effects of NGO-Union Relationships on Corporate Responsibility: The Case of the Swedish Clean Clothes Campaign', *Journal of Business Ethics*, Vol. 64, No. 3, pp. 303–316.

Electricity Supply Association of Australia [ESAA] (2012), 'Comparing Australian and International Energy Prices' (ESAA, Melbourne).

European Commission (2011), 'Communication from the Commission to the European Parliament, The Council, The European Economic and Social Committee and The Committee of the Regions: A Roadmap for Moving to a Competitive Low Carbon Economy in 2050. COM(2011) 112 final' (European Commission, Brussels).

European Commission (2014), *2030 Framework for Climate Change and Energy* (European Commission, Brussels).

European Environment Agency (2013), 'Total Primary Energy Intensity (CSI 028/ENER 017) – Assessment published Feb 2013' (European Environment Agency, Copenhagen).

European Union (2009), 'Decision No 406/2009/EC of the European Parliament and of the Council of 23 April 2009 on the effort of Member States to Reduce their Greenhouse Gas Emissions to Meet the Community's Greenhouse Gas Emission Reduction Commitments up to 2020' (European Union, Brussels).

Falkner, R. (2003), 'Private Environmental Governance and International Relations: Exploring the Links', *Global Environmental Politics*, Vol. 3, No. 2, pp. 72–87.

Fombrun, C., Gardberg, N. and Barnett, M. (2000), 'Opportunity Platforms and Safety Nets: Corporate Citizenship and Reputational Risk', *Business and Society Review*, Vol. 105, No. 1, pp. 85–106.

Freeman, R., Harrison, J., Wicks, A. and Parmar, B. (2010), *Stakeholder Theory: The State of the Art* (Cambridge University Press, Cambridge).

Gouldson, A. (2004), 'Risk, Regulation and the Right to Know: Exploring the Impacts of Access to Information on the Governance of Environmental Risks in the UK', *Sustainable Development*, Vol. 12, pp. 136–149.

Gouldson, A. and Bebbington, J. (2007), 'Corporations and the Governance of Environmental Risks', *Environment and Planning C*, Vol. 25, No. 1, pp. 4–20.

Gouldson, A. and Murphy, J. (1998), *Regulatory Realities: The Implementation and Impact of Industrial Environmental Regulation* (Earthscan, London).

Gouldson, A. and Sullivan, R. (2007), 'Corporate Environmentalism: Tracing the Links between Policies and Performance Using Corporate Reports and Public Registers', *Business Strategy and the Environment*, Vol. 16, pp. 1–11.

Gouldson, A. and Sullivan, R. (2013), 'Long-term Corporate Climate Change Targets: What Could They Deliver?', *Environmental Science & Policy*, Vol. 27, pp. 1–10.

Gouldson, A. and Sullivan, R. (2014), 'Understanding the Governance of Corporations: An Examination of the Factors Shaping UK Supermarket Strategies on Climate Change', *Environment and Planning A*, Vol. 46, No. 12, pp. 2972–2990.

Gouldson, A., Lidskog, R. and Wester-Herber, M. (2007), 'The Battle for Hearts and Minds? Evolutions in Organizational Approaches to Environmental Risk Communication', *Environment and Planning C*, Vol. 25, No. 1, pp. 56–72.

Groupe Auchan (2012), *Sustainable Ideas, Progressive Ideas. 2011 Sustainability Report* (Groupe Auchan, Paris).

Groupe Auchan (2014), *2013 Annual and Corporate & Social Responsibility Report* (Groupe Auchan, Paris).

Groupe Casino (2003), *Sustainable Development Report 2002* (Groupe Casino, Saint Etienne).

Groupe Casino (2004), *Sustainable Development Report 2003* (Groupe Casino, Saint Etienne).

Groupe Casino (2005), *Sustainable Development Report 2004* (Groupe Casino, Saint Etienne).

Groupe Casino (2006), *Sustainable Development Report 2005* (Groupe Casino, Saint Etienne).

Groupe Casino (2007), *Sustainable Development Report 2006* (Groupe Casino, Saint Etienne).

Groupe Casino (2008), *Sustainable Development Report 2007* (Groupe Casino, Saint Etienne).

Groupe Casino (2009), *Sustainable Development Facts and Figures 2008* (Groupe Casino, Saint Etienne).

Groupe Casino (2010), *Sustainable Development Facts and Figures 2009* (Groupe Casino, Saint Etienne).

Groupe Casino (2011), *2010 Annual Report and Social Responsibility Performance* (Groupe Casino, Saint Etienne).

Groupe Casino (2012), *2011 Annual Report and Social Responsibility Performance* (Groupe Casino, Saint Etienne).

Groupe Casino (2013), *2012 Annual and Corporate Social Responsibility Performance Report* (Groupe Casino, Saint Etienne).

Groupe Casino (2014), *2013 Annual and Corporate Social Responsibility Performance Report* (Groupe Casino, Saint Etienne).

Hemingway, C. (2005), 'Personal Values as a Catalyst for Corporate Social Entrepreneurship', *Journal of Business Ethics*, Vol. 60, No. 3, pp. 233–249.

Hertel-Fernandez, A. (2019), *State Capture: How Conservative Activists, Big Businesses, and Wealthy Donors Reshaped the American States – and the Nation* (Oxford University Press, Oxford).

Home Depot (2012), 'Home Depot Inc's Response to the 2012 CDP Survey' (Home Depot, Atlanta).

Home Depot (2014), *2014 Sustainability Report* (Home Depot, Atlanta).

Howard, J. (1997), 'Safeguarding the Future: Australia's Response to Climate Change. Statement by The Prime Minister of Australia, The Hon. John Howard MP, 20 November 1997'.

ICF International (2012), *An International Comparison of Energy and Climate Change Policies Impacting Energy Intensive Industries in Selected Countries. Report Prepared for Department for Business Innovation & Skills, 11 July 2012* (ICF, London).

IGD (2012). 'China's Grocery Market Overtakes the US as Biggest in the World. Press Release. 2 April 2012' (IGD, London).

IGD (2013). 'Press Release: China's Grocery Market Reaches US$1trillion. 5 June 2013' (IGD, London).

Institute for European Environmental Policy [IEEP] and Natural Resources Defense Council (NRDC) (2008), *Climate Change and Sustainable Energy Policies in Europe and the United States* (IEEP, Brussels; NRDC, Washington DC).

Intergovernmental Panel on Climate Change [IPCC] (2007), *Climate Change 2007: Synthesis Report – Summary for Policymakers* (IPCC, Geneva).

IPCC (2014a), *Climate Change 2014: Mitigation of Climate Change. Contribution of Working Group III to the Fifth Assessment Report of the Intergovernmental Panel on Climate Change* (Cambridge University Press, Cambridge).

IPCC (2014b), *Climate Change 2014: Synthesis Report. Contribution of Working Groups I, II and III to the Fifth Assessment Report of the Intergovernmental Panel on Climate Change* (IPCC, Geneva).

IPCC (2018), *Global Warming of 1.5°C. An IPCC Special Report on the Impacts of Global Warming of 1.5°C Above Pre-industrial Levels and Related Global Greenhouse Gas Emission Pathways, in the Context of Strengthening the Global Response to the Threat of Climate Change, Sustainable Development, and Efforts to Eradicate Poverty* (IPCC, Geneva).

J Sainsbury (2003), *Environment Report 2003* (J Sainsbury, London).

J Sainsbury (2004), *CSR 2004: Corporate Social Responsibility* (J Sainsbury, London).

J Sainsbury (2005), *Corporate Responsibility Report 2005* (J Sainsbury, London).

J Sainsbury (2006), *Corporate Responsibility Report 2006* (J Sainsbury, London).

J Sainsbury (2007), *Corporate Responsibility Report 2007* (J Sainsbury, London).

J Sainsbury (2008), *Corporate Responsibility Report 2008* (J Sainsbury, London).

J Sainsbury (2009), *Corporate Responsibility Report 2009* (J Sainsbury, London).

J Sainsbury (2010), *Corporate Responsibility Report 2010* (J Sainsbury, London).

J Sainsbury (2011a), *Sainsbury's Corporate Responsibility Report 2011* (J Sainsbury, London).

J Sainsbury (2011b), *Sainsbury's 20 by 20 Sustainability Plan* (J Sainsbury, London).

J Sainsbury (2013), *20 x 20. Our Progress so Far...November 2013* (J Sainsbury, London).

J Sainsbury (2014), 'Operational Carbon' (J Sainsbury, London).

Japan Chain Stores Association [JCSA] (2014), 'Efforts to Prevent Global Warming' (JCSA, Tokyo).

Japan Franchise Chain Association [JFCA] (2014), 'JFCA's Efforts for Environmental Protection' (JCSA, Tokyo).

Jeffery, L., Alexander, R., Hare, B., Rocha, M., Schaeffer, M., Höhne, N., Fekete, H., van Breevoort, P. and Blok, K. (2015), *How Close are INDCs to 2 and 1.5°C Pathways? Climate Action Tracker Update. 1 September 2015* (Carbon Tracker, London).

Jessop, B. (2004), 'Hollowing Out the Nation-state and Multilevel Governance', in Kennett, P. (2004), *A Handbook of Comparative Social Policy* (Cheltenham, Edward Elgar), pp. 11–25.

John Lewis Partnership (2007), *Corporate Social Responsibility in an Enterprising Partnership* (John Lewis Partnership, London).

John Lewis Partnership (2009), *A Natural Progression: Corporate Social Responsibility Report 2009* (John Lewis Partnership, London).

John Lewis Partnership (2010), *A Shared Passion: Corporate Social Responsibility Report 2010* (John Lewis Partnership, London).

John Lewis Partnership (2011), *A Clear View: Corporate Social Responsibility Report 2011* (John Lewis Partnership, London).

John Lewis Partnership (2012), *Sustainability Report 2012* (John Lewis Partnership, London).

John Lewis Partnership (2014), *John Lewis Partnership Sustainability Review 2014* (John Lewis Partnership, London).

Jordan, A., Huitema, D., Hildén, M., van Asselt, H., Rayner, T., Schoenefeld, J., Tosun, J., Forster, J. and Boasson, E. (2015), 'Emergence of Polycentric Climate Governance and its Future Prospects', *Nature Climate Change*, Vol. 5, pp. 977–982.

Keidanren (2013), *Keidanren's Commitment to a Low Carbon Society. January 17, 2013* (Keidranen, Tokyo).

Kelemen, D. and Vogel, D. (2010), 'Trading Places: The Role of the United States and the European Union in International Environmental Politics', *Comparative Political Studies*, Vol. 43, pp. 427–456.

Knox-Hayes, J. and Levy, D. (2011), 'The Politics of Carbon Disclosure as Climate Governance', *Strategic Organization*, Vol. 9, pp. 91–99.

Kolominskas, C. and Sullivan, R. (2004), 'Improving Cleaner Production through Pollutant Release and Transfer Register Reporting Processes', *Journal of Cleaner Production*, Vol. 12, pp. 713–724.

Kooiman, J. (2003), *Governing as Governance* (Sage, London).

Kotter, J. and Heskett, J. (1992), *Corporate Culture and Performance* (The Free Press, New York).

Kroger (2007), *2007 Public Responsibilities Report* (Kroger Co, Cincinatti, OH).

Kroger (2009), *2009 Sustainability Report* (Kroger Co, Cincinatti, OH).

Kroger (2012a), 'Kroger's Response to the 2012 CDP Survey' (Kroger Co, Cincinatti, OH).

Kroger (2012b), *2012 Sustainability Report* (Kroger Co, Cincinatti, OH).

Kroger (2014), *2014 Sustainability Report* (Kroger Co, Cincinatti, OH).

Kuroda, K., Sullivan, R. and Gouldson, A. (2014), 'Climate Change: Why UK and Japanese Retailers Respond Differently', *Ethical Corporation*, 18 April 2014.

Lane, S. (2013), 'Combet Confirms Carbon Trading Tax Cut on Hold', *ABC News*, 10 May 2013.

Leahy, T., (2007), 'Tesco, Carbon and the Consumer'. Speech to a Forum for the Future and Tesco event, London, 18 January 2007.

Leviston, Z., Price, J., Malkin, S. and McCrea, R. (2014), *Fourth Annual Survey of Australian Attitudes to Climate Change: Interim report* (CSIRO, Perth).

Levy, D. and Newell, P. (eds.) (2005), *The Business of Global Environmental Governance*, (MIT Press, Cambridge).

Lewis, M. (2018), *The Fifth Risk: Undoing Democracy* (W.W. Norton & Co., London).

Lidl (2014), 'Climate-friendly Logistics Centers' (Lidl, Baden-Württemberg).

Lowe's (2012), 'Lowe's Response to the 2012 CDP Survey' (Lowe's Companies Inc, Mooresville, NC).

Lowe's (2014), *Lowe's 2013 Social Responsibility Report* (Lowe's Companies Inc, Mooresville, NC)

Luce, S. (2013), *Global Retail Report* (UNI Global Union, Nyon, Switzerland).

Marks and Spencer (2004), *Corporate Social Responsibility Report 2003/04* (Marks and Spencer, London).

Marks and Spencer (2007), *How We Do Business: 2007 Report* (Marks and Spencer, London).

Marks and Spencer (2008), *How We Do Business Report 2008* (Marks and Spencer, London).

Marks and Spencer (2009), *How We Do Business Report 2009* (Marks and Spencer, London).

Marks and Spencer (2014), *Plan A Report 2014* (Marks and Spencer, London).

Metro AG (2002) *Sustainability in Trading 2002* (Metro AG, Dusseldorf).

Metro Group (2004), *Sustainability Report 2004* (Metro Group, Dusseldorf).

Metro Group (2006), *Sustainability Report 2006* (Metro Group, Dusseldorf).

Metro Group (2008), *Sustainability Report 2007* (Metro Group, Dusseldorf).

Metro Group (2009), *Sustainability. Progress 2008 Key Data and Targets* (Metro Group, Dusseldorf).

Metro Group (2011a), *Sustainability. Progress Report 2010* (Metro Group, Dusseldorf).

Metro Group (2011b), 'Metro Group's Response to the 2011 CDP Survey' (Metro Group, Dusseldorf).

Metro Group (2012a), *Sustainability. Progress Report 2011* (Metro Group, Dusseldorf).

Metro Group (2012b), 'Metro Group's Response to the 2012 CDP Survey' (Metro Group, Dusseldorf).

Metro Group (2013a), *Sustainability Report 2012* (Metro Group, Dusseldorf).

Metro Group (2013b), *Metro Group Carbon Footprint* (Metro Group, Dusseldorf).

Milne, M. and Grubnic, S. (eds.) (2011), *Accounting, Auditing & Accountability Journal (Special Issue: Climate Change, Greenhouse Gas Accounting, Auditing and Accountability)*, Vol. 24, No. 8.

Monbiot, G. (2000), *Captive State: The Corporate Takeover of Britain* (Pan Macmillan, London).

Monks, R. and Minnow, N. (2011), *Corporate Governance* (John Wiley and Sons, Chichester).

Morrison, J. (2014), *The Social License: How to Keep Your Organization Legitimate* (Palgrave, London).

Ostrom, E. (2005), *Understanding Institutional Diversity* (Princeton University Press, Princeton, NJ).

Ostrom, E. (2010) 'Beyond Markets and States: Polycentric Governance of Complex Economic Systems', *American Economic Review*, Vol. 100, pp. 1–33.

Paavola, J., Gouldson, A. and Kluvankova-Oravska, T. (2009), 'Institutions, Ecosystems and the Interplay of Actors, Scales, Frameworks and Regimes in the Governance of Biodiversity', *Environmental Policy and Governance*, Vol. 19, No. 3, pp. 148–158.

Pattberg, P. (2007), *Private Institutions and Global Governance: The New Politics of Environmental Sustainability* (Edward Elgar, Cheltenham).

Pfeifer, S. and Sullivan, R. (2008), 'Public Policy, Institutional Investors and Climate Change: A UK Case-study', *Climatic Change*, Vol. 89, pp. 245–262.

Pinske, J. and Kolk, A. (2009), *International Business and Climate Change* (Routledge, Abingdon).

PWC (2014), *Two Degrees of Separation: Ambition and Reality. Low Carbon Economy Index 2014* (PWC, London).

PWC (2019), *Emissions Relapse. The Low Carbon Economy Index 2019* (PWC, London).

Ravasi, D. and Schultz, M. (2006), 'Responding to Organisational Identity Threats: Exploring the Role of Organizational Culture', *Academy of Management Journal*, Vol. 49, No. 3, pp. 433–458.

Retail Industry Leaders Association [RILA] (2012), *2012 Retail Sustainability Report* (RILA, Arlington, VA).

Retail Industry Leaders Association [RILA] (2013), *2013 Retail Sustainability Report* (RILA, Arlington, VA).

REWE Group (2009), *REWE Group Corporate Carbon Footprint* (REWE Group, Cologne).

REWE Group (2011), *Sustainability Report 2009/2010* (REWE Group, Cologne).

REWE Group (2013), *Raus aus der Nische: Nachhaltigkeitsbericht 2011/2012* (REWE Group, Cologne).

REWE Group (2014a), 'Carbon Footprint' (REWE Group, Cologne).

REWE Group (2014b), 'Refrigerants – Reducing Climate-Relevant Emissions' (REWE Group, Cologne).

REWE Group (2014c), 'REWE Green Building' (REWE Group, Cologne).

REWE Group (2014d), 'Logistics' (REWE Group, Cologne).

RobecoSAM (2013), *Measuring Country Intangibles* (RobecoSAM, Zurich).

Sabatier, P. and Jenkins-Smith, H. (1999), 'The Advocacy Coalition Framework: An Assessment', in Sabatier, P. (ed.), *Theories of the Policy Process* (Westview Press, Boulder, CO).

Safeway (2014), 'Planet: Climate and Energy' (Safeway, Pleasanton, CA).

Schaltegger, S. (1997), 'Information Costs, Quality of Information and Stakeholder Involvement: The Necessity of International Standards of Ecological Accounting', *Eco-Management and Auditing*, Vol. 4, pp. 87–97.

Schein, E. (2010), *Organizational Culture and Leadership* (4th ed.) (John Wiley and Sons, San Francisco).

Schoenberger, E. (2000), 'Creating the Corporate World', in Sheppard, E. and Barnes, T (eds.), *A Companion to Economic Geography* (Blackwell, Oxford).

Seven & i Holdings (2007a), *CSR Report 2007* (Seven & i Holdings Ltd, Tokyo).

Seven & i Holdings (2007b), 'Seven & i's Response to the 2007 CDP Survey' (Seven & i Holdings Ltd, Tokyo).

Seven & i Holdings (2008), *CSR Report 2008* (Seven & i Holdings Ltd, Tokyo).

Seven & i Holdings (2009a), *CSR Report 2009* (Seven & i Holdings Ltd, Tokyo).

Seven & i Holdings (2009b), 'Seven & i's Response to the 2009 CDP Survey' (Seven & i Holdings Ltd, Tokyo).

Seven & i Holdings (2010), *CSR Report 2010* (Seven & i Holdings Ltd, Tokyo).

Seven & i Holdings (2011), *CSR Report 2011* (Seven & i Holdings Ltd, Tokyo).

Seven & i Holdings (2012a), *CSR Report 2012* (Seven & i Holdings Ltd, Tokyo).

Seven & i Holdings (2012b), 'Seven & i's Response to the 2012 CDP Survey' (Seven & i Holdings Ltd, Tokyo).

Seven & i Holdings (2013), *CSR Report 2013* (Seven & i Holdings Ltd, Tokyo).

Stern, N. (2006) *Stern Review: The Economics of Climate Change* (Cambridge University Press, Cambridge).

Stern, N. and Taylor, C. (2010), *What do the Appendices to the Copenhagen Accord Tell us about Global Greenhouse Gas Emissions and the Prospects for Avoiding a Rise in Global Average Temperature of More than 2°C? Policy Paper. March 2010* (Centre for Climate Change Economics and Policy, London).

Strange, S. (1996), *The Retreat of the State: The Diffusion of Power in the World Economy* (Cambridge University Press, Cambridge).

Sullivan, R. (2005), *Rethinking Voluntary Approaches in Environmental Policy* (Edward Elgar, Cheltenham, UK).

Sullivan, R. (2006), 'Greenhouse Challenge Plus: A New Departure or More of the Same?', *Environmental and Planning Law Journal*, Vol. 23, No. 1, pp. 60–73.

Sullivan, R. (2007), 'Australia Country Case-Study. Human Development Report Office Occasional Paper 2007/61 (Human Development Report 2008/2008)' (United Nations Development Programme, New York).

Sullivan, R. (ed.) (2008), *Corporate Responses to Climate Change* (Greenleaf Publishing, Sheffield).

Sullivan, R. (2009), 'The Management of Greenhouse Gas Emissions in Large European Companies', *Corporate Social Responsibility and Environmental Management*, Vol. 16, No. 6, pp. 301–309.

Sullivan, R. (2010), 'An Assessment of the Climate Change Policies and Performance of Large European Companies', *Climate Policy*, Vol. 10, pp. 38–50.

Sullivan, R. (2011a), *Valuing Corporate Responsibility: How Do Investors Really Use Corporate Responsibility Information?* (Greenleaf Publishing, Sheffield).

Sullivan, R. (2011b), *Investment-Grade Climate Change Policy: Financing the Transition to the Low-Carbon Economy* (Institutional Investors Group on Climate Change, London).

Sullivan, R. and Blyth, W. (2006), *Climate Change Policy Uncertainty and the Electricity Industry: Implications and Unintended Consequences. Chatham House Briefing Paper EEDP BP 06/02* (Chatham House, London).

Sullivan, R. and Gouldson, A. (2007), 'Pollutant Release and Transfer Registers: Examining the Value of Government-Led Reporting on Corporate Environmental Performance', *Corporate Social Responsibility and Environmental Management*, Vol. 14, pp. 263–273.

Sullivan, R. and Gouldson, A. (2012), 'Does Voluntary Carbon Reporting Meet Investors' Needs?', *Journal of Cleaner Production*, Vol. 36, pp. 60–67.

Sullivan, R. and Gouldson, A. (2013), 'Ten Years of Corporate Action on Climate Change: What Do We Have To Show For It?', *Energy Policy*, Vol. 60, pp. 733–740.

Sullivan, R. and Gouldson, A. (2016), 'Comparing the Climate Change Actions, Targets and Performance of UK and US Retailers', *CSR and Environmental Management*, Vol. 23, No. 3, pp. 129–139, May/June 2016.

Sullivan, R. and Gouldson, A. (2017), 'The Governance of Corporate Responses to Climate Change: An International Comparison', *Business Strategy and the Environment*, Vol. 26, pp. 413–425.

Sullivan, R. and Pfeifer, S. (2009), 'Moving the Capital Markets: The EU Emissions Trading Scheme', *Journal of Corporate Citizenship*, No. 33, pp. 87–96.

Sullivan, R. and Woods, I. (2000), 'Using Emission Factors to Characterise Heavy Metal Emissions from Sewage Sludge Incinerators in Australia', *Atmospheric Environment*, Vol. 34, No. 26, pp. 4571–4577.

Sullivan, R., Martindale, W., Feller, E., Pirovska, M. and Elliott, R. (2019), *Fiduciary Duty in the 21st Century: Final Report* (The Generation Foundation, PRI and UNEP FI, London).

Sustainable Development Commission [SDC] (2008), *Green, Healthy and Fair: A Review of the Government's Role in Supporting Sustainable Supermarket Food* (SDC, London).

Target (2012), 'Target's Response to the 2012 CDP Survey' (Target Corporation, Minneapolis).

Target (2014), 'Target's Response to the 2014 CDP Survey' (Target Corporation, Minneapolis).

Tesco (2007), *Corporate Responsibility Review 2007* (Tesco, Cheshunt).

Tesco (2010), *Corporate Responsibility Report 2010* (Tesco, Cheshunt).

Tesco (2013), *Tesco and Society Report 2013* (Tesco, Cheshunt).

Tesco (2014a), *Tesco and Society Report 2014* (Tesco, Cheshunt).

Tesco (2014b), 'Reducing Our Impact on the Environment' (Tesco, Cheshunt).

Unerman, J. and Bennett, M. (2004), 'Increased Stakeholder Dialogue and the Internet: Towards Greater Corporate Accountability or Reinforcing Capitalist Hegemony?', *Accounting, Organizations and Society*, Vol. 29, No. 7, pp. 685–707.

United Nations Environment Programme [UNEP] (2019), *Emissions Gap Report 2019* (UNEP, Nairobi).

US Climate Action Network (2014), 'Who's On Board With The Copenhagen Accord?' 23 September 2015 (US Climate Action Network, Washington DC).

US Department of Agriculture [USDA] Foreign Agricultural Service (2012), *France: Grocery Retail. GAIN (Global Agricultural Information Network) Report, 24 September 2012. Report No. FR9116* (USDA, Paris).

US Department of Agriculture [USDA] Foreign Agricultural Service (2013), *Germany: Retail Foods. GAIN (Global Agricultural Information Network) Report, 22 August 2013. Report No. GM13031* (USDA, Berlin).

US White House, Office of the Press Secretary (2014), 'U.S.-China Joint Announcement on Climate Change. Beijing, China, 12 November 2014' (US White House, Washington DC).

Waitrose (2008), *How We Stack Up: Corporate Social Responsibility Report 2008* (John Lewis Partnership, London).

Walmart (2009a), *2009 Global Sustainability Report* (Walmart, Bentonville, AR).

Walmart (2009b), 'Walmart's Response to the 2009 CDP Survey' (Walmart, Bentonville, AR).

Walmart (2014), *2014 Global Responsibility Report* (Walmart, Bentonville, AR).

Wernerfelt, B. (1984), 'The Resource Based View of the Firm', *Strategic Management Journal*, Vol. 5, No. 2, pp. 171–180.

Wernerfelt, B. (1995). 'The Resource Based View of the Firm: Ten Years After'. *Strategic Management Journal*, Vol. 16, No. 3, pp. 171–174.

Wesfarmers (2009), *Sustainability Report 2009* (Wesfarmers, Perth).

Wesfarmers (2010), *Sustainability Report 2010* (Wesfarmers, Perth).

Wesfarmers (2011), *Sustainability Report 2011* (Wesfarmers, Perth).

Wesfarmers (2012a), *Sustainability Report 2012* (Wesfarmers, Perth).

Wesfarmers (2012b), 'Wesfarmers' Response to the 2012 CDP Survey' (Wesfarmers, Perth).

Wesfarmers (2013), *Sustainability Report 2013* (Wesfarmers, Perth).

Wm Morrison (2009), *Corporate Social Responsibility Report 2008/09* (Wm Morrison, Bradford).

Wm Morrison (2013), *Corporate Social Responsibility Review 2012/13* (Wm Morrison, Bradford).

Woolworths (2005), *Corporate Social Responsibility Report 2005* (Woolworths, Sydney).

Woolworths (2007), *Sustainability Strategy 2007–2015* (Woolworths, Sydney).

Woolworths (2008), *Corporate Responsibility Report 2008* (Woolworths, Sydney).

Woolworths (2009), *Corporate Responsibility Report 2009* (Woolworths, Sydney).

Woolworths (2010), *Corporate Responsibility Report 2010* (Woolworths, Sydney).

Woolworths (2011a), *Corporate Responsibility Report 2011* (Woolworths, Sydney).

Woolworths (2011b), 'Woolworth's Response to the 2011 CDP Survey' (Woolworths, Sydney).

Woolworths (2012a), *Corporate Responsibility Report 2012* (Woolworths, Sydney).

Woolworths (2012b), 'Woolworth's Response to the 2012 CDP Survey' (Woolworths, Sydney).

Woolworths (2013), *Corporate Responsibility Report 2013* (Woolworths, Sydney).

Wrigley, N., Guy, C. and Lowe, M. (2002), 'Urban Regeneration, Social Inclusion and Large Store Development: The Seacroft Development in Context', *Urban Studies*, Vol. 39, No. 11, pp. 2101–2114.

Wurzel, R., Zito, A. and Jordan, A. (2013), *Environmental Governance in Europe: A Comparative Analysis of New Environmental Policy Instruments* (Edward Elgar, Cheltenham).

Index

Page numbers in bold refer to information in tables, italics to figures.

Printed in the United States
By Bookmasters